LUTHER DISCOVERS
THE GOSPEL

Luther Discovers the Gospel

NEW LIGHT UPON LUTHER'S WAY
FROM MEDIEVAL CATHOLICISM
TO EVANGELICAL FAITH

By
Uuras Saarnivaara, Ph. D., Th. D.

Wipf and Stock Publishers
EUGENE, OREGON

Wipf and Stock Publishers
199 West 8th Avenue, Suite 3
Eugene, Oregon 97401

Luther Discovers the Gospel
New Light Upon Luther's Way from Medieval Catholicism to Evangelical Faith
By Saarnivaara, Uuras
Copyright© January, 1951 Concordia Publishing House
ISBN: 1-59244-147-5
Publication date: February, 2003 .
Previously published by Concordia Publishing House, January, 1951 .

This book is dedicated to my father, Dean Emil Edward Saarnivaara of Finland, whose counsels and prayers have been a great blessing to me, and whose support and encouragement have meant much in my theological work; and to the memory of my beloved mother, Olga Maria Saarnivaara (b. Linna), who passed to glory when I was writing this book in the summer of 1943

Preface

WHEN the Protestant world in 1883 celebrated the quadricentennial of the birth of Martin Luther, the great Reformer, a new interest was aroused in the study of his life and teachings. This interest received a new impetus from the crushing defeat brought by the First World War to the optimistic dreams of the "liberal" theology and culture. Men felt that they needed a more vital Christianity and a deeper theology than the anemic one which had been prevalent up to the great war. This seemed to be offered by the great Reformer, who had found a way to the fountains of divine grace and life and who had rediscovered the Gospel, which helps men to be reconciled with God and to come into a living experience of fellowship with Him.

The revitalized Luther research, which was now growing into a "Luther renaissance," was not satisfied with studying the teachings of the Reformer. It felt that its first task was to give answer to the question: How did Luther himself find a way to a fellowship with God and to an evangelical faith? It was convinced that his teaching of the way of salvation could be rightly understood only in the light of his own struggles and experiences. An intense study was therefore focused on the early life of Luther and on his way to the evangelistic faith. More prominent scholars studied this question, and more studies were published on it than on any other topic in the field of Luther research.

It was, however, unfortunate that many of the men who tried to trace the path of the Reformer from the Roman Catholic to an evangelical faith had received their theological schooling in the "liberal" tradition of the pre-war theology. The result was very strange indeed: These students of Luther came to the conclusion that Luther's early teaching of justification, which was somewhat related to the ideas of the prevalent liberal theology, was his real teaching and that he himself did not remember correctly his own struggles and his path to the light of the Gospel. He made gross mistakes — these theologians said — in relating his own way and the decisive turning points of it. Only now his way to the evangelical faith and the doctrine he taught was rightly understood.

Some theologians doubted these results, and no wonder. It is hard to believe that a man like Luther could have given such a wrong picture of the great turning points of his spiritual pilgrimage.

The present writer became aware of the unreliability of the prevalent "results" of recent Luther research while making an investigation into the issue in preparing a dissertation in partial fulfillment of the requirements for the degree of Doctor of Philosophy at the Divinity School of the University of Chicago. The present volume is an outcome of this investigation. It tries to show what was Luther's path to a living fellowship with God and to a participation in the grace through which he gained the joyful assurance that he was acceptable to God. The author is confident that his interpretation is more reliable than the prevalent one because it respects Luther's own statements on the matter and takes into account all the other documents and facts which throw light on the issue.

The author feels himself under obligation to express his gratitude to Professor Wilhelm Pauck, his adviser, for valuable guidance and constructive criticism during the course of the work. Professors William Arndt and Theodore Graebner of Concordia Theological Seminary, St. Louis, Mo., have also read the manuscript. The author wishes to express his appreciation for their co-operation and kind appraisal of the work. He also wishes to express his sincere thanks to Professor Joseph Sittler of the Chicago Theological Seminary and Rev. Walter J. Kukkonen of Superior, Wis., for their help in preparing the English text of the book.

The present study was published in 1947 in the Finnish language in Helsinki, Finland.

UURAS SAARNIVAARA

Contents

PREFACE	IX
INTRODUCTION	XIII

PART ONE

The Significance of Augustine, Staupitz, and Scripture in Luther's Search for Truth and Salvation

1. AUGUSTINE'S CONCEPTION OF THE SINNER'S SALVATION AND ITS RELATION TO LUTHER'S MATURE TEACHING	3
Augustine on the Justification of a Sinner	3
The Mature Luther on Justification and Augustine	9
2. STAUPITZ AND LUTHER	19
Luther's Testimony Concerning Staupitz	19
The Teachings of Staupitz	22
3. LUTHER'S DISCOVERY IN THE TOWER	35
Luther's Own Testimonies	35
The Meaning of the Tower Discovery	39

PART TWO

Luther's Early Conception of Justification and His Final Discovery of the Gospel

4. THE MARGINAL NOTES ON AUGUSTINE AND LOMBARD AND THE DECISIVE INFLUENCE OF STAUPITZ	53
5. LUTHER'S FIRST LECTURES ON THE PSALMS, 1513–1515	59

6. LUTHER'S LECTURES ON ROMANS, 1515–1516	74
7. LUTHER'S CONCEPTION OF JUSTIFICATION IN 1517–1518	88
8. LUTHER'S "TOWER EXPERIENCE" AT THE END OF THE YEAR 1518	92
SUMMARY AND CONCLUSION	120
NOTES	127
BIBLIOGRAPHY	136
INDEX	143

Introduction

When Luther was seeking a way to peace with God and to an assurance of salvation, he had to find a solution to the greatest issue of life and death in man's personal relation to God: How can man, cut off from God by his sins and guilt, become acceptable to Him and enter into a living personal fellowship with Him? In Luther's life this quest for salvation was made up of two subissues: first, how could he find peace for his conscience through the forgiveness of sins? — second, how could he become justified or righteous in the sight of the Holy One? As we shall see, Luther did not face these two sides, or aspects, at the same time. There was an interval of several years between the two crises of his life in which he found a solution to each of them.

In order to understand the young Luther's struggles in his search for a solution of these problems, we have to recall the three interpretations of the way to righteousness which were offered to him. The term "justified" or "righteous" were used from Old Testament times to signify the state in which man is acceptable to God, to live in fellowship with Him.

First of all, Luther met the view, common to the religious people of all times, that God looks with favor upon those who have done their best to obey His Law. He rewards good deeds and punishes evil deeds. In theological terminology this is called the "active" view of justification, because, according to it, man is acceptable to God if he is just in his activity, that is, if his behavior and walk conforms to the demands of the divine Law.

Secondly, Luther learned to know the official teaching of the Roman Church, according to which man is justified by being healed from his sin-sickness and corruption so that he is able to love God and his fellow men and thus to fulfill the Law. He becomes acceptable to God, or righteous in His sight, by this grace-wrought renewal *and* the ensuing righteous activity, or good works. Thus, man is both "passive" and "active" in justification: he receives the healing and renewing grace as a gift of God, that is, "passively," but he is "active" in doing good works by which he merits eternal life. This healing of sin-sickness does not take place in a moment, and time is needed for doing the good works by which eternal life is merited. Therefore justification is a gradual process of becoming righteous through a co-operation between divine grace and the efforts of man. God forgives what is lacking in man's righteousness, not imputing his remaining weaknesses and sins for guilt. — The justifying and forgiving grace is poured, or infused, into the soul of man in the sacraments, and it empowers him to merit eternal bliss through good works.

The third way to righteousness was taught by the Apostle Paul and other New Testament writers. According to it man is justified through faith, by the redemption which is in Christ Jesus. The man whose sins are pardoned and to whom God does not impute sin is righteous in His sight for the sake of the blood and the atoning sacrifice of Christ, in which he puts his trust in faith (Rom. 3:23-25; 5:3-6; Heb. 10:14). The justifying faith is a living faith, through which man lives in communion with God and bears good fruits in love and obedience. Christ dwells through faith in the believer's heart, and, constrained by the love of Christ, he no longer lives to himself, but to Him who has loved him and given Himself for him. He is a new creature, created in Christ Jesus for good works. But these good works are only the fruit, not the foundation of justification (2 Cor. 5:15; Eph. 2:8-10; Gal. 2:20; 5:6; etc.). In this kind of justification man is wholly "passive": as an unmerited gift he receives the forgiveness of sins; and he is reckoned righteous, righteousness is imputed to him, not on the grounds of anything that is in him, but for the sake of Christ's finished work alone.

Until the period of recent Luther research Protestant theology

Introduction

unanimously regarded Luther's doctrine of justification as belonging to the Pauline type. It was the discovery of this way to righteousness before God that made him the Reformer. But in recent times the renowned Luther scholar Karl Holl, and to some extent also his students, tried to prove that Luther's teaching of justification was of the second type, although in an improved and purified form, and that he found his way to peace with God in the way shown by this doctrine. One's conception of Luther's path to the evangelical faith depends, as we shall see, on the stand he takes on this primary issue. More than that, the solution of this problem involves and affects deeply his whole understanding of sinful man's way to God and of the Christian life in general.

Consequently, we have a twofold task in our study: first, to ascertain the contents of Luther's mature teaching of justification and his discovery of the Gospel, and second, to trace his own way to the peace of conscience and to the rediscovery of the Gospel, and the dates of these events. Luther himself states several times that particularly Augustine (bishop of Hippo, died 430 A. D.), Johann von Staupitz (general vicar, or superintendent, of the Augustinian Friars in Germany, to whom Luther belonged), and the Scriptures gave him help and guidance in his search for truth and peace. Our study will, therefore, take place in the form of an investigation of the influences of these three factors on his spiritual and theological development.

PART ONE

The Significance of Augustine, Staupitz and Scripture in Luther's Search for Truth and Salvation

1

Augustine's Conception of the Sinner's Salvation and Its Relation to Luther's Mature Teaching

AUGUSTINE ON THE JUSTIFICATION OF A SINNER

AUGUSTINE deals with the justification of a sinner, for the most part, in those writings which he produced in his struggle against the Pelagian and semi-Pelagian heresies. It was mainly by these writings of the Bishop of Hippo that Luther was influenced in the time he was seeking for the truth.

What was the conception of the salvation of a sinner Luther found in these writings?

According to Augustine man's true relationship to God is one of humble subjection and trust. In the fall into sin, however, man set himself against God, arrogantly desiring to be his own lord and master. This rebellion so corrupted his nature that man no longer seeks his "good" — his joy and happiness — in God, but rather in created things. Consequently he has no freedom of will in spiritual matters, but his spirit is in bondage to his flesh, ignorance darkens his soul, and death hounds him. All because of sin.[1]

The Law of God demands willing and spontaneous obedience. Man, however, is corrupt in just this respect that he is unwilling and unable to fulfill this demand. The Law reveals to him his weakness, his sinfulness, and the sickness of his will. When such a man hears the good news of the grace of God, a hunger and thirst for salvation are created in him. He begins to pray for pardon and the renewing grace which will enable him to love God and his neighbor.

God bestows this grace upon man in Baptism. Those who have fallen from baptismal grace are restored through repentance (conversion). In this manner man has his ailing nature and will cured and is enabled to seek his "good" in God and to obey His Commandments. More than the mere example of Christ is necessary. The divine Spirit must recreate the heart of man in order to free his will. The Spirit "inspires us with a good desire which replaces the evil lust (in other words, sheds abroad love in our hearts)."[2]

"The human will is divinely aided in the pursuit of righteousness, so that . . . man receives the Holy Spirit, by whose gift there springs up in his mind even in the present state a delight in and a love for that supreme and unchangeable good which is God."[3]

"It is the Spirit of grace that does it, in order to restore in us the image of God in which we are created. All sin, indeed, is contrary to nature, and it is grace that heals it."[4]

In this way "nature is repaired by grace."[5] By inspiring in us a good will and acceptable activity, the life-giving Spirit writes the Law of God in our hearts.[6]

Augustine teaches that all love is acquisitive. Directed downward, to the created things of the world, it is a sinful love, *cupiditas*, or concupiscence. But when it is directed upward, to seek its "good" in God, it is a Christian love, *caritas* (charity). Man, as created by God, possessed charity, but in the Fall his desires and strivings, that is, his love, took a turn downward. It began to seek its "good" in the creature world. Only the renewing grace of God can restore the original and proper direction to man's desire and striving.

In so far as cupidity holds sway in man, he is sinful and unrighteous. On the other hand, when love, or *caritas*, controls his heart, he is righteous.[7]

The sinful man is also guilty in the sight of God and the object of His holy displeasure. However, it is not so much his guilt as his depravity and the "sickness" of his nature that is decisive in his relationship to God. The principal work of the grace of God is, therefore, to heal his nature. This healing, or renewal, Augustine calls renovation, vivification, regeneration, and justification. To him justification, therefore, means that man is made righteous in regard to his will and behavior. As a result he has the right attitude toward God and is willing and able to do good works, empowered by the divine grace and Spirit. So it is that God "heals the spiritually sick or quickens the dead, that is, justifies the ungodly."[8] Again and again Augustine quotes statements from Paul concerning justification and the "righteousness of God." In each case he interprets them to mean this "restoring" righteousness, or the healing of human nature.

The thoughts of Augustine as expressed in his treatise *On the Spirit and the Letter* are particularly pertinent to our study. It was this treatise to which Luther makes reference in his account of his discovery of the evangelical conception of the phrase "the righteousness of God." In his exposition of Rom. 1:17, "the righteousness of God is manifested [in the Gospel]," Augustine states:

"He does not say, the righteousness of man or the righteousness of his will, but the 'righteousness of God' — meaning not that whereby He Himself is righteous, but that with which He endows man when He justifies the ungodly. . . .

"'Being justified freely by His grace.' It is not, therefore, by the Law nor by their own will that they are justified; but they are justified freely by God's grace — not that the justification takes place without our will; but our will is shown to be weak by the Law, that grace may heal its infirmity, and thus healed, it may fulfill the Law."[9]

The fact that justifying grace is gratuitous means that there are no antecedent merits:

"Now it is freely or gratuitously that he is justified thereby, that is, he has no previous merits of his own with which to earn this favor, 'otherwise grace is no more grace,' since it is bestowed on us, not because we have done good works, but that we might be able to do them — in other words, not because we have fulfilled, but in order that we might be able to fulfill the Law." [10]

In his discussion of the contrast between the righteousness of the Law and the righteousness of grace, Augustine makes the following statements:

"For what else does the phrase 'being justified' signify than 'being made righteous' by Him who justifies the ungodly man that he may become a godly one instead." [11]

"Justification is the inscription of the Law into the hearts of men by the Holy Spirit." [12]

The words "divine aid makes possible for us the achievement of righteousness" imply that righteousness is not something that is received complete, but rather a gradual process of becoming righteous in which the renewed will of man co-operates with the grace of God. Man must constantly long and pray for righteousness or justification, that God may give him greater power to turn away from the world and to fulfill the Law in love and obedience. Concerning this, Augustine remarks further in the same treatise:

"The faith which hungers and thirsts after righteousness progresses therein through the daily renewal of the inner man. Its hope is that in eternal life this hunger and thirst will be satisfied.

" 'The righteousness of God' is used in the sense of our being made righteous by His gift, and 'the salvation of the Lord' in the sense that we are saved by Him, and 'the faith of Jesus Christ' to mean that He makes us believers in Him. This is the righteousness of God which He not only teaches by the precept of His Law, but also bestows upon us by the gift of His Spirit." [13]

Man never becomes absolutely righteous in this life, but he is always advancing toward the goal of righteousness, which is perfect renewal. In fact, it is dangerous for him to consider himself to be completely justified.

"Regardless of the righteousness he has, [he should not] presume that he has it of himself, but from the grace of God, who justifies him, and [he must] continue to hunger and thirst after righteousness from Him who is the living bread. . . . He works justification in His saints in such a manner that He may continue to have something to impart to them in a liberal manner when they ask, and something to forgive them in His mercy when they confess." [14]

Since justification is a gradual process of "healing" of human nature, and since the believer has more sin than righteousness, it is essential for him to continue to remain humble. There must be no cessation in his feeling and confessing of his sins or in his accusing and condemning himself. "Sin cannot remain unpunished. . . . It must be punished either by man or God, who judges." [15] "It is a commendation of grace that none of us counts his own righteousness as something. For this is the righteousness of God, given to us by God that it might be ours." [16]

When Augustine says that a Christian is "at the same time righteous and sinful" *(simul iustus et peccator)*, he means that love *(caritas)* does not have full dominion in his heart and life. There is in him a continual warfare between love and cupidity. His flesh entices him to seek pleasure in the world. His renewed will, empowered by love, seeks and desires the treasures of heaven and finds its pleasure in them. Although his evil lust is being mortified, it is not yet dead, but continues to live and move in his flesh. At times it even causes him to fall into sin. During his earthly pilgrimage, therefore, the believer can never say: "I am righteous" *(iustus sum)* and mean "I am not a sinner" *(peccator non sum)*. He is called righteous because of the beginning of righteousness in him. In reality, however, he has only started on his course toward righteousness. As yet he is an admixture of good and evil, spirituality and carnality, love and evil lust. His righteousness increases, or ought to increase, daily until it reaches its perfection in the future life, but in this life the believer is "justified in part" only.[17] He is "to some degree righteous, to some degree sinful."[18]

While the believer is being purified, God forgives the sins which remain in him and does not impute them as guilt. Thus the Christian has a twofold grace: (1) forgiveness and (2) justification or renewal. Sin "remains as to its activity, but it passes away as to its guilt. Not that it ceases to exist, but it is not imputed."[19]

The fact that justification continues to be throughout this life in its initial stages, means that forgiveness of sins must constitute the greater portion of the salvation of man. The gracious imputation of God takes care of the greater portion which is concupiscence and thereby fills up what the Christian lacks in love.

"Even though our righteousness is true in so far as it is related to the genuine good, yet in this life it is of such a nature that it consists in the remission of sins rather than in the perfection of virtues."[20]

Augustine never tires of stressing that man is saved by grace alone. "It is only by unmerited mercy that any is redeemed, and only well-deserved judgment when any is condemned."[21] Before the foundation of the world God decided to save some out of the "mass of perdition," which is mankind, and to let others receive their just condemnation. This was His eternal decree of predestination.

"For it is grace alone that separates the redeemed from the lost, all having been involved in the common perdition through their common origin."[22]

Theologians are generally agreed that the Augustinian conception of salvation is a combination of Christian and Neo-Platonic ideas. As Anders Nygren especially has pointed out,[23] the Neoplatonism of Augustine is apparent particularly in his concept of love. Man's sin consists in his love for and trust in earthly things; therefore his salvation and righteousness consist in his turning to seek his happiness in God and things of heaven. His conversion is, therefore, largely a "change of taste," as Karl Holl puts it.²⁴ His primary concern in his conversion is not to find a merciful God through the remission of sins, but to receive from God a new "taste" and power to subdue his evil lust and to pursue heavenly things.

THE MATURE LUTHER ON JUSTIFICATION AND AUGUSTINE

There are several characteristic aspects of Luther's conception of justification and sanctification:

1. Man is justified wholly for the sake of Christ. Christ has "merited" and prepared for him the righteousness which God bestows upon him:

"Your righteousness is Christ, who was made a curse for you and who redeemed you from the curse of the Law." ²⁵

"The fruit and benefit of His sacrifice and ministry are the forgiveness of sins and justification." ²⁶

2. Man is justified by the imputation, or reckoning, of this righteousness and pardon, prepared and earned by Christ, to the benefit of the sinner:

"Our glory is to know assuredly that our righteousness is divine, as God does not impute sins. Our righteousness is nothing but imputation." "It consists not in any merits, but in the favor and imputation of God through faith." ²⁷

"A Christian is not he who has no sin, but to whom God does not impute sin for the sake of faith in Christ. . . . We have good reason, therefore, to impress often upon our minds the forgiveness of sins and the imputation of righteousness for Christ's sake." ²⁸

The passive righteousness which the believing sinner receives as a free gift through the gracious imputation of God is identical

---

²⁴ "Augustins innere Entwicklung," *Gesammelte Aufsaetze zur Kirchengeschichte* III, 85. — A "change of taste" is, of course, a part of all true conversion, taking the word in the wider sense. Augustine also taught that appropriation of the forgiveness belongs to conversion, but the primary thing for him was, in any case, renewal in the sense of a "change of taste" and a change in the direction of desire and love.

with the forgiveness of sins. This acquittal from guilt makes him acceptable to God and blameless in His sight. "I know nothing of the Law and sin, and for the sake of this passive righteousness there will follow in death the righteousness of the flesh" (body).[29]

3. Man is justified when he appropriates and receives by faith this forgiveness of imputed righteousness. Faith does not justify because it is a new quality in man, but because it lays hold of the promise of grace and relies on the mercy of God alone.

"We are justified by faith alone, because faith alone appropriates the victory of Christ. In so far as you believe, you have it." [30]

"Faith does not justify as a work, but because it apprehends the mercy revealed in Christ." [31]

4. Justification is not a gradual process, but an instantaneous act of God whereby He pronounces the sinner free from his guilt. The sinner appropriates at once full forgiveness and complete righteousness in Christ. From that moment he is totally righteous, that is, guiltless and blameless, in the sight of God. God does not want to see or remember his sins for the sake of the propitiation performed by His Son.

"Justification does not take place through works, but by faith alone, without any works, and not piecemeal, but completely at once *(nit mit stucken, szondern auff eynem hauffen)*. The testament, that is, the Gospel promise, includes everything in itself: justification, salvation, inheritance, and blessing. It is appropriated by faith completely at once, not piecemeal *(gantz auff eynn mal, nit stucklich besessen durch den glawben)*. Truly it is plain, then, that faith alone brings such good things of God, that is, justification and salvation, and makes us instantaneously, not gradually, children and heirs, who then freely do good works of all kinds." [32]

The foundation and "content" of justification is the finished work of Christ, the propitiation, or reconciliation, which He has accomplished for all mankind for the forgiveness of its sins. Imputation and faith indicate the manner and way in which this grace becomes the sinner's personal possession.

5. Luther teaches that God not only forgives sins and reckons the sinner righteous, but He also renews him and makes him righteous in his heart and life. This renewal, however, he distinguishes as the second part of God's work of salvation. At times he calls it the "second justification," the "first justification" being the justification by faith, by the imputation of God. On the basis of Rom. 5:15 he calls these two "grace" *(gratia)* and "gift" *(donum).* "Grace," or the righteousness of faith, is given completely and instantaneously, while the "gift," or the Holy Spirit and the renewal effected by Him, is given gradually.

"Between grace and gift there is this difference: Grace means properly the love and favor of God which He has in Himself toward us.... Grace accomplishes such great things that we are reckoned completely and perfectly righteous before God, for this grace is not divided or broken up into parts, as are the gifts. God takes us entirely and perfectly into His favor for the sake of Christ....

"The gifts and the Spirit increase in us each day and are not yet perfect, so that there remain in us evil lust and sin." [33]

The problem involving the relationship between justification and renewal, or sanctification, was taken up repeatedly in the academic disputations held at Wittenberg from 1536 to 1543. Luther defined the relationship between these two gifts of God as follows:

"God purifies nations, that is, reckons them purified, because they have faith, although in reality they are sinners.... For He first cleanses by imputation, then *(deinde)* He gives the Holy Spirit, by whom we are cleansed in regard to our substance. Faith purifies through the remission of sins; the Holy Spirit purifies by His effect." [34]

In the course of these disputations the question arose repeatedly whether the renewal effected by the Spirit and the new obedience belong to justification along with imputation. In 1536, for example, it was asked "whether we are justified through the imputation of faith alone or also through some kind of change in us" *(etiam aliqua nostra mutatione).* Luther answered by definitely denying that any possible changes in us belong to justification *(non concurrit ad iustificationem)*. The question was further asked whether the new obedience of believers belongs to justification. Luther replied:

"Justification is the remission of sins, which has to do only with faith. Justification means the forgiveness of sins. Obedience is not involved in it at all, because Paul received forgiveness of sins prior to his obedience. Paul was not righteous in any other way than through the remission of sins. . . . That partial righteousness, namely, of obedience, does not justify." [35]

The ultimate purpose of God's saving work is the complete renewal of man, but it is not realized until in eternity. Here on earth this renewal, or the "second righteousness," the righteousness of life, never progresses beyond a mere beginning. The believer, therefore, must put his trust before God in the forgiveness of sins and in the imputed righteousness alone.

6. The right distinction between the Law and the Gospel is bound inseparably with the doctrine of justification. Luther laid strong emphasis on the Pauline teaching that the sole "spiritual" office, or task, of the Law is to work conviction of sin in the human heart and so to prepare him for the reception of the Gospel grace. The Gospel does not demand any works of man. It is the good news of Christ and of His redemptive and atoning work in behalf of sinners. Through it God reveals and imparts the forgiveness of sins or the justifying grace. By means of the Gospel, as proclaimed by the ministry of reconciliation on earth, God pronounces His gracious imputation, His judgment of acquittal. The fulfillment of the Law through love toward God and fellow men does not belong to justification.

In renewal, or the "second righteousness," the relationship of the believer to the Law is different. The Law is written in his heart by the Spirit of God, so that he is renewed, or transformed, both inwardly and outwardly to conform to the Law. He is, as Luther sometimes put it, sanctified according to the first and the second table of the Law. The Spirit creates in him the right attitude toward God and his fellow men. This renewal, however, will be complete only in the future life. In one of the Wittenberg disputations Luther states:

"That exaction [of the Law] ceases in Christ through the remission of sins and the divine imputation, when we believe in Him who fulfilled the Law, for it is the will of God that the Law be fulfilled. In addition He gives us the Holy Spirit in order that we may begin here to fulfill it. In the life to come we shall be like Christ, who fulfilled the Law." [35]

"We are free from the Law, which ceases with Christ in a twofold sense: first imputatively, when sins against the Law are no longer imputed to me, but are remitted for the sake of the most precious blood of the spotless Lamb, Jesus Christ, my Lord; then, by expurgation, when the Holy Spirit is given me, so that, having received Him, I begin to hate from my heart everything that offends His name and to follow good work." [36]

"It is faith alone that accomplishes this that all sins are remitted to us and the entire Decalog fulfilled therein, because faith alone gives me Christ, who is the fulfillment and the end of the Law. What else does faith bestow? It imparts and brings with it the Holy Spirit, from whom all good works flow." [37]

These statements show that Luther does not include in justification before God the actual fulfillment of the Law in the believer. That belongs to the fruits of justifying faith or to sanctification.[38]

---

[38] Karl Holl avers that Luther does not teach justification by the mere imputation of righteousness and by the non-imputation of sins for the sake of Christ. According to Holl, Luther teaches that "God justifies the sinner whom He Himself makes righteous and because He makes him righteous." Thus, justification means renewal, and only after God has renewed man and made him righteous, He declares him righteous. The actual basis of the divine judgment which justifies is not the merit of Christ, but the renewal of man (Holl, *Gesammelte Aufsaetze zur Kirchengeschichte* III (Tuebingen, 1928), pp. 530 ff.; "Das Ergaebnis der Auseinandersetzung ueber die Rechtfertigungslehre," *Neue Kirchliche Zeitschrift*, 1924, p. 47). — As we shall see, Holl is in the main right if we consider Luther's early teaching of justification. But he

Justification and renewal must be clearly distinguished but not separated from each other. God never justifies man without renewing him, and He never renews him without justifying him. Justification, or forgiveness, has the primary position according to both logic and the Christian experience. But faith implies in itself a new attitude toward God, true knowledge of God, trust and confidence in His goodness and mercy, and also a willingness to obey Him. It is impossible to believe in the grace of God and to lay hold by faith of the forgiveness of sins, unless God gives His Spirit to man and effects this change in him.

A comparison of the teachings of Augustine and Luther on justification clearly shows that they interpret this term quite differently. Augustine means by justification the renewal or gradual transformation of man into the image of God. Luther understands by it the forgiveness of sins, the imputation of righteousness for the sake of Christ.

Both Augustine and Luther teach that the salvation of man consists in two gifts of God, forgiveness and renewal. Both also believe that the renewal of man is the work of the Spirit of God, received through faith. Further, both teach that divine grace and non-imputation supply or supplement what is lacking in the human righteousness of life. Finally, both speak of repentance, humility, confession of sins, self-accusation, prayer for mercy as divinely effected prerequisites of the initial and continual reception of grace. At first glance it appears that the difference is one of terminology alone:

Augustine: Justification = renewal; non-imputation of sins is its supplement.

Luther: Justification = non-imputation of sins and imputation of righteousness; renewal is its fruit or the second work of God.

Modern exegesis agrees rather unanimously that Luther is cor-

---

is wrong with regard to his final teaching. Holl's mistake was that he interpreted Luther in the light of his early, or pre-Reformation, writings and did not see the difference between these and his Reformation statements regarding justification.

rect in his interpretation of the Pauline teaching on justification and that Augustine errs in his exposition. The Latin word *iustificare* = *iustum facere*, to make righteous, led Augustine astray. Because of his inadequate knowledge of Greek, he failed to realize that *dikaioo* means "I declare righteous, or acquit." [39]

According to Augustine, conversion means a "change of taste," or a man's turning to seek his joy and happiness in God. This he is enabled to do by the renewal of his will, which the Spirit of God alone can effect. When the divine call creates within him the desire for such a turning to God, his first task is to confess his depravity and weakness and to pray that God would renew his heart and will.

In the usage of Luther the primary meaning of the term "conversion" is appropriation of the forgiveness of sins. When the Law brings man to a conviction of his sins, his great concern and burden is his *guilt*, because of which he is under the holy displeasure and wrath of God. He needs to pray for forgiveness and mercy and to accept the Gospel promise of forgiveness of sins in Christ. Having appropriated this grace, he is righteous before God, or justified, and has peace with God. As a natural and necessary fruit of this faith he begins to live a new life of obedience to God, loving God and his fellow men as God has loved and loves him.[40]

Augustine also knows of the forgiveness of sins as a great and necessary gift of God, but he does not think of conversion primarily as an appropriation of the remission of sins, but as a change in the objects of love and longing.

For Augustine the "passivity" of justification implies that the renewal of the will is the work of God and not an accomplishment of man. For Luther it means that man receives remission of sins

---

[39] Paul Feine, *Die Erneuerung des Paulinischen Christentums durch Luther* (Leipzig, 1903), pp. 24 ff.

[40] A "change of taste" is part of conversion also according to Luther. The converted man loves what he before hated and seeks what he before despised. But this is the fruit of the justifying faith, or the work of the gift of the Holy Spirit, not justification itself.

or the imputed righteousness as a free gift. However, man is not entirely "passive" in renewal. Although it also is entirely the work of God, yet it is in a sense "active" righteousness, involving, as it does, the matter of attitude and activity on the part of man.

Augustine believes that man is justified by fulfilling the Law of God through the power which he receives from God. Luther teaches that man must first be justified and possess by faith the perfect fulfillment of the Law accomplished by Christ. Only then is it possible for him to endeavor to fulfill the Law in love and obedience. Their understanding of the relationship between the Law and the Gospel is, therefore, altogether different. According to Augustine the Law drives man to Christ to seek power for the fulfillment of the Law in love and obedience. According to Luther the Law drives man to Christ to receive from Him a perfect fulfillment already accomplished. The fulfillment of the Law in love will follow as the fruit of this faith.

Consequently the nature and character of the Christian faith and life receive a different interpretation in the two systems. In the Augustinian system justification is a future attainment. The Christian must strive for it continually, always abiding in humility, condemning himself, praying for mercy, and endeavoring to conform to the Law of God. In the Lutheran system justification and possession of righteousness is a present reality. No human effort is necessary for its attainment, since it is received in all its fullness by faith in the promise of the Gospel. Only in sanctification continuous striving is necessary.

It follows that sorrow because of the presence of sin and the lack of righteousness is characteristic of the Augustinian faith, while joy over salvation and the perfect righteousness in Christ has the central place in the Lutheran faith. To be sure, both Augustine and Luther acknowledge the need for continuing humility and consciousness of sin. In the Augustinian faith the presence of sin tends, however, to destroy the certainty of salvation, since sinfulness is equivalent to lack of righteousness; while in the Lutheran faith sin does not (though it never ceases to create temptations and doubts), or should not, cause doubt as to the complete and fully sufficient righteousness of Christ.

Finally, Augustine and Luther agree as to the necessity of an unceasing struggle against sin and a daily mortification of the flesh. Luther takes this "good fight of faith" just as earnestly and seriously as Augustine; but in this warfare he is free from the necessity of anxious examination of himself and his growth in holiness. Such liberty Luther considers essential for successful advancement in this struggle.

Augustine belonged to the Catholic Church. His conception of salvation was Catholic and not evangelical. The Roman Church has developed and modified his doctrine of justification at numerous points, but basically it is still Augustinian. The Catholics have always agreed with Augustine that justification is not a non-imputation of sins and an imputation of the righteousness of Christ. In its essence it is the renewal of man by grace which enables him to become righteous by doing good works in love, for man is justified by faith which works through love. The emphasis is on love, which is the actual content of justification.[41]

Protestant theologians have too regularly permitted the similarities between the teaching of Augustine and Luther to lead them astray. Matter of fact is that there exists a deep gulf between the teachings

---

[41] In the Council of Trent (1545—63) the Roman Catholic Church defined its doctrine against the Reformation teaching as well as against certain views within its own fold. Justification was declared to consist of two things: (1) Infusion of the *"habitus,"* or quality, of charity into the heart of man, and (2) the forgiveness of sins. The former was understood to constitute the real essence of justification, with the latter as a supplement. The Lutheran (and Calvinistic) doctrine of justification (imputation of the righteousness of Christ, or forgiveness of sins, excluding renewal or the inherent grace and love) was anathematized (Session VI, can. xi; Philip Schaff, *The Creeds of Christendom*, Vol. II, New York, 1919, p. 112). Cf. Hans Rueckert, *Die Rechtfertigungslehre auf dem Tridentinischen Konzil* (Bonn, 1925), pp. 101—108, 114 f., 123 ff., 220—227, 256—261.

of Augustine and Luther on justification. To speak of justification by grace through faith for Christ's sake and of the non-imputation of sins that remain is not necessarily to have the Lutheran conception of justification. These phrases go together also with the Augustinian view, according to which justification is a process of becoming righteous. It is not simply a difference in emphasis that separates the teachings of these two men. The real difference lies in the conception of the nature and content of justification.[42] It is this criterion that must be applied in the estimation of Luther's teachings in the various phases of his development.

---

[42] F. Kattenbusch, "Die vier Formen des Rechtfertigungsgedankens," *Zeitschrift fuer systematische Theologie*, XI (1933), pp. 28 ff., says that the Augustinian-Catholic conception is "reparatory" *(reparatorisch)* — man is "repaired" into his original condition by the abolition of sin itself — while the Lutheran conception is "reconciliatory" *(rekonziliatorisch)*. Justification consists of both forgiveness, or removal of guilt, and the gradual removal of corruption through renewal. According to Kattenbusch, Lutheran Orthodoxy deviated from the teaching of Luther by adopting a "compensatory" *(kompensatorisch)* view of justification: the vicarious sacrifice of Christ is imputed to the sinner for justification, which means only the removal of guilt for the sake of Christ. — Kattenbusch is an example of the rather prevalent confusion of the Augustinian and Lutheran conceptions of justification, which is common particularly in modern liberal theology. In reality, Lutheran Orthodoxy understood Luther quite correctly.

2

Staupitz and Luther

LUTHER'S TESTIMONIES CONCERNING STAUPITZ

In 1518 Luther added to his book on indulgences (*Resolutiones disputationum de indulgentium virtute*) a letter of dedication to his friend and superior Johann von Staupitz. This letter throws much light upon the development of Luther in the question of repentance. We shall quote the most significant portion of its text.[43]

"I remember, Reverend Father, that in one of your delightful and wholesome talks, by which the Lord Jesus usually gives me wonderful comfort, mention was made of the word 'repentance' (*poenitentia*). I received your word as coming from Heaven when you said that repentance is not genuine unless it begins with a love of righteousness and God (*ab amore iustitiae et Dei incipit*), and that what the torturers consider to be the end and consummation of repentance is rather its beginning (*esse potius principium poenitentiae, quod illis finis et consummatio censetur*).

"This your word fixed itself in me like a sharp arrow of the mighty. At once I began to compare it with the Scripture texts on repentance. And, behold, I had a most pleasant surprise! Statements from all sides began to sound forth in harmony and, plainly smiling, to gather around this dictum, so that the word 'repentance' which had been the most bitter term in the whole Bible to me, although with great zeal I pretended even before God and tried to exert myself to a feigned and forced love *(fictum coactumque amorem exprimere conarer)*, now became to me the most sweet and pleasant-sounding word of all. For thus the commands of God become sweet when we understand that they are to be read not only in books, but in the wounds of the sweetest Savior.

"Afterwards it happened that through studying learned men, who render great service in teaching us Greek and Hebrew, I discovered that the original meaning of this Greek word *metanoia*, from *meta* and *nous*, which mean 'afterwards' and 'mind,' is coming to one's right mind again. . . . Next I saw, as I made progress, that *metanoia* means not only 'after' and 'mind,' but can also be derived from 'over again' and signify a change of mind and affection, indicating, it seems, not only the fact, but also the method of the change, that is, the grace of God. For such transformation of the mind, namely, repentance that is genuine, is mentioned quite frequently in the Scriptures.

"Clinging fast to this conclusion, I took courage to think that they were wrong who attributed so much to the works of penance that almost nothing was left of repentance except stiff satisfactions and a most laborious confession. They were led astray by the Latin word *'poenitentiam agere,'* which sounds as if it referred to an action rather than to a change of mind and in no wise does justice to the Greek *metanoein*."

Election and predestination was another problem in which Luther credits the counsels of Staupitz with delivering him from difficult doubts and afflictions. In a letter to the Count of Mansfeld in 1542 Luther says: "If Doctor Staupitz, or rather, God through Doctor Staupitz, had not helped me out of it, I would have succumbed therein and been in hell long ago." [44]

The great *Commentary on Genesis* contains the statement: "Listen to the Incarnate Son, He offers Himself freely. Then predestination follows immediately. With these words Staupitz consoled me, Why do you torture yourself with such speculations? Look to the

Staupitz and Luther

wounds of Christ and His blood, shed for you. From them shines the predestination." [45]

Several similar statements by Luther are to be found in his *Table Talks*.

"Once I complained to my Staupitz of the fact that predestination is so sublime. He answered me: Predestination is understood and found in the wounds of Christ, nowhere else, because it is written, listen to this. . . ." [46]

"Doctor Staupitz said to me, when one desires to discuss predestination, it is better not to think of it, but to start with the wounds of Christ and to set Christ carefully before the mind's eye. That takes care of predestination — God foresaw the suffering of His Son for sinners. He who believes in Him is predestined, he who does not believe is not." [47]

According to Luther it was Staupitz who helped him take the right attitude also toward temptations, afflictions, and pangs of conscience in general.

"When I first started in the monastery," Luther says, "it happened that I was always sad and sorrowful and unable to throw off this sad state of mind. I consulted Doctor Staupitz because of my problem and confessed to him, a man whom I mention with pleasure, revealing to him my horrible and terrifying thoughts. When he had heard me, he said: 'Don't you know, Martin, that such a temptation is useful and necessary for you, for thereby God does not train you at random. You shall see that He will use you as His servant to accomplish great things.'" [48]

In this particular case, as the letter reveals, Luther was tortured by a feeling of his own sinfulness and had pangs of conscience on account of fairly insignificant and trivial things.[49]

Luther himself gave similar counsel to Weller: "This temptation is more necessary for you than food and drink." [50]

Luther stated in a letter to Staupitz (dated September 17, 1523) that through him he had come to know the Gospel grace in a personal way: "We ought not to forget you and be ungrateful to you, through whom the light of the Gospel began to shine the first time from darkness into our heart." [51] Another time Luther said that Staupitz had "started the doctrine" by pointing him to the incarnate Son of God.[52]

THE TEACHINGS OF STAUPITZ

Luther study of today is in a position to estimate more correctly the influence of Staupitz on Luther than was possible three decades ago. In addition to the sermons and works of Staupitz, we have a thorough study of the relations between him and Luther.[53] Heretofore, however, sufficient use of this material has not been made in the general presentations of the development of Luther.

According to Staupitz, the conversion and justification of man cannot occur without the experience of contrition or anguish and terror for sin in the heart *(dolor cordis)*. To those who have in their hearts such a sorrow over sin God extends an invitation to come to Him. Weeping over their sins and putting their trust in the promise of God declared to them in absolution, they arise from their fallen state. The efficacy of the suffering and death of Christ is revealed in these sacraments. Therefore they convey to men the justifying grace of God.[54]

Staupitz seems to know of no "works of disposition" by means of which man should make himself ready for divine grace. Only sorrow over sin and trust in the divine promise of forgiveness in absolution, he points out, are necessary for salvation.

True penitence or contrition flows out of love for God and righteousness. Without such love it is impossible for man to hate and detest sin and to repent of it. An important problem in the doctrine of repentance, therefore, is the question of the origin, or creation, of such love in the human heart. Is it the result of man's own efforts, or is it the work of God?

Staupitz answers the question by saying that such a love for God and His will is the product of two factors: (1) the revelation of the love of God in Christ and in His suffering for men, and (2) the work of the Holy Spirit in the heart of man. "The love of Christ kindles the spirit of the bride (that is, man)." [55] "Love for God is created by the revelation of the love of God toward us." [56]

According to the medieval Catholic teaching, renewal through the infusion of grace is primary in justification. Remission of sins is of secondary significance and dependent upon the renewal. Certain statements of Staupitz give the impression that he understood forgiveness and justification to be synonymous terms almost in the spirit of evangelical theology.

"We are . . . justified by the blood of Christ, for that innocent blood was shed for the remission of our sins. . . . Thus reborn by the blood of Christ . . . we possess heaven although we live on earth." [57]

Man is saved by the twofold grace of God, the forgiveness of sins and the renewal by the indwelling Spirit. Time and again Staupitz emphasizes the fact that man cannot by any efforts of his own become "worthy" of the divine grace.[58] True, a "preparation" or "disposition" is necessary for the reception of grace. As long as man does not know his sin and guilt, but lives with the presumption of his own goodness, he is unfit for grace. By working in him contrition, sorrow, and distress over sin, God draws man to Christ. Thereby the cross of Christ receives all credit and glory for salvation.[59]

In counseling concerning the sacrament of penance, Staupitz was careful to guard against causing men to rely upon their frequent and painful confessions. He said that the main thing was trust *(vertrawen)* in the grace of God, which is revealed in Christ and sealed by the sure promise of the Savior Himself.[60]

To experience anguish on account of the punishment of sin is not real repentance. Staupitz calls it "gallows repentance" *(Galgenrew, attritio)*. True repentance is created by a contemplation of the vicarious sufferings of Christ for our sins. The love of God as revealed in these sufferings of the Savior kindles in our hearts a love for Him and a true sorrow over sin and all that is displeasing to Him.[61]

We are incapable of "perfect" repentance. All that is in us is deficient. However, repentance, or contrition, can be "true" although it is not perfect. God is satisfied even with imperfect repentance as long as it is sincere. The "repentance" and merit of Christ supplies what is lacking in our repentance.[62] Equally unnecessary is a complete enumeration of sins in confession. Staupitz advised that only sins against the Ten Commandments should be confessed in penance. Other sins should be confessed only if they cause particular trouble to the conscience, and if the "erring conscience" cannot find comfort in any other way.[63]

Staupitz's booklet on predestination [64] contains a statement to the effect that divine election is the initial grace which makes man acceptable to God. In bestowing upon man His grace which makes him acceptable, God merely executes His gracious decree of election to make man His living and justified child.[65]

Agony and affliction of the heart and conscience on account of sin are a necessary part of repentance and salvation. They are not signs of the wrath of God, but of His love and election. Those whom God has chosen for salvation have such agonies; therefore they should not despair, but humbly bear them, praying for the mercy of God.[66] Furthermore, such afflictions and pangs of conscience must not be feared because they are the means by which man becomes like Christ *(conformitas Christi)*. Christ suffered more afflictions than any man, and those who shall inherit salvation must conform to their Master and follow in His footsteps of suffering. Also from this point of view afflictions are a sign of election.[67]

Since it is impossible for man to know the hidden divine decree of election as regards himself or others, he must be content to hold to the "present predestination." By this Staupitz means the love and grace of God which is revealed in the Cross of Christ and imparted to man in the Sacraments and the Word of God. That is the only way in which one is able to overcome the afflictions caused by the problem of predestination.

This brief summary of the teachings of Staupitz shows that he was very close to the evangelical understanding of salvation. True, he still had many Catholic ideas, but we have overlooked them, since we are interested in his practical teaching of salvation. It is evident that by a diligent study of the Bible and the teachings of Augustine, Bernhard, and others, he was freed from the Catholic "retributory order of salvation" *(Vergeltungsordnung)*, according to which man had to work out his own salvation through his merits, assisted more or less by divine grace. Staupitz taught salvation by grace alone and led sinners to put their trust solely in the crucified Savior.[68]

One of the main problems of practical Christianity with which Luther wrestled was that of repentance. The "last great Occamist," Gabriel Biel of Tuebingen, and the "Gabrielists" of Erfurt taught that man is able to repent of his sins by his natural powers. It is within his power to love God above all and to detest sin out of love for righteousness. A number of Nominalists, like Johann Paltz of Erfurt in his *Celifodina*, held the view that God may be satisfied with an imperfect repentance flowing from fear of punishment and hope of reward, provided that there is also a hatred of sin, a desire

---

[68] There has been disagreement among scholars as to which "school" of medieval theology and piety Staupitz belonged. Otto Scheel, *Martin Luther. Vom Katholizismus zur Reformation* II (Tuebingen, 1930), pp. 366, 645, and Eino Sormunen, *Jumalan armo* II. Luther (Helsinki, 1934), p. 33, hold that he was a Thomist, who had been influenced by the Augustinian doctrine of grace and predestination; Heinrich Boehmer, *Der junge Luther* (Gotha, 1925), p. 102, asserts that he was a Thomist and an adherent of the *devotio moderna* or the late medieval Netherlandish Mysticism (to which, e. g., Thomas à Kempis belonged). — Staupitz cannot be identified with any school of theology. To be sure, he was closer to Aquinas than Scotus or Occam, and he had received influences from Augustine and Bernhard and others, but it is probable that his greatest influence came from the Word of God, which he as an Augustinian studied diligently as the rules of the order required. — The fact that he favored Thomism over Nominalism (Occamism) is evident from his successful attempt to make the new university of Wittenberg (established 1502) a proponent of Thomism.

to be free from it, and a longing to repent perfectly. The sensitive conscience of Luther, however, could not be satisfied with such easygoing religion and partial repentance. He looked upon it as a temptation of the devil to think that one should not take sin too seriously or be too strict and thorough in confession.[69]

Luther put forth his best in his attempt to love God and to repent of his sins out of love for righteousness, but he discovered that it was impossible. At its best his repentance was only attrition, "gallows repentance," which was caused by fear of punishment and desire for reward. Occasionally, perhaps, he thought his repentance was satisfactory, but the ultimate result was monotonously the same, failure. It is revealing to read his own description of his

---

[69] Several scholars hold that Staupitz was in the bonds of the Catholic retributory order of salvation. So, e. g., Scheel, *op. cit.* II, 373, 386, and T. Bohlin, *Gudstro och kristustro hos Luther* (Uppsala, 1927), p. 39. Such a conception, however, receives no support from the statements of Staupitz himself. Scheel, *op. cit.* II, pp. 367, 383 f., asserts, moreover, that in the teachings of Staupitz and his counsels to Luther there is nothing new that cannot be found in the writings of other Catholics of that time. — It may be possible to gather similar statements from the works of various teachers of the medieval Catholic Church, but it proves nothing. Here it is a question of the counsels of Staupitz in the context of his general teaching of the way of salvation and of their significance to Luther. Undoubtedly Staupitz's teaching of salvation was more evangelical and Scriptural than that of the Catholics in general. We cannot agree with Boehmer when he states (*op. cit.*, p. 100) that Staupitz was "very far from the Gospel" (*Evangelium sehr fern*). On the contrary, he was *very near* the Gospel.

André Jundt, *Le developpement de la pensée religieuse de Luther jusque'en 1517 d'apres des document inedites* (Paris, 1906), p. 56, expresses a view which is quite prevalent when he says that Staupitz was no theologian, but a man of practical piety. Therefore he was not able to influence the doctrinal views of Luther, who received from him only his practical piety. — It is true that Staupitz's help to Luther was primarily a matter of practical piety. Yet, a study of the writings and sermons of Staupitz shows that he was enough of a theologian to possess definite doctrinal convictions, which strongly influenced the theological development of Luther.

Staupitz and Luther

struggles for a good conscience through a complete confession of his sin and for freedom from his evil desires:

"As a monk I labored under the impression that my salvation was lost when I experienced fleshly desire, that is, evil lust, sensuality, anger, hatred, envy, and so forth, toward my brother. I tried many things. I confessed daily . . . but I made no progress — the evil lust of the flesh continued to return. As a result I did not find peace, but only further vexed myself." [70]

In 1518, in a letter to Staupitz, Luther wrote: "I tried to exert myself to a feigned and forced love." But he found out that this was no way to peace and assurance of salvation. His soul remained in doubt and uncertainty. As he arose from confession, this thought arose within him: "I was not sufficiently sorry for my sins. I forgot something in my confession." [71] The medieval Church required in penance a detailed confession of sins. Sins that were overlooked in confession had to be confessed as soon as possible after their recollection. Especially the Nominalists, who dominated in the University of Erfurt, were particularly strict at this point.[72]

The unevangelical form of absolution, which was in use among the Augustinian monks, was another serious obstacle in Luther's path as he sought peace of soul. We have, preserved in his writings, the following form of absolution: "I absolve thee from thy sins

---

72 Cf. A. V. Mueller, *Luthers Werdegang bis zum Turmerlebnis* (Gotha, 1920), p. 35; Y. J. E. Alanen, *Das Gewissen bei Luther* (Helsinki, 1936), p. 115; Scheel, *op. cit.* II, 276. — The Catholic C. Feckes, *Die Rechtfertigungslehre des Gabriel Biel* (Muenster i. w., 1925), p. 147, admits that it was the teaching of repentance of Biel and his requirement of perfect contrition that was one of the main causes of the difficulties of Luther. Feckes, however, is entirely wrong in saying that Luther gave up the "sacrament of repentance" altogether, being content with mere "inner repentance." One can see this if he only considers the chapter on Confession in Luther's *Small Catechism*. See also, e. g., H. Fuglsang-Damgaard's study "Die Wiederbelebung der Privatbeichte im Lichte der Auffassung Luthers," *Zeitschrift fuer systematische Theologie*, 1934, pp. 458 ff., and U. Saarnivaara, *The Power of the Keys* (Hancock, Mich., 1945).

through the merits of our Lord Jesus Christ, for the sake of the contrition of thy heart, the confession of thy mouth, and the intercession of the saints."[73] Since contrition and confession are here mentioned alongside the merits of Christ as the basis of absolution, this form of absolution is actually conditional. Forgiveness depends on the adequacy of the contrition and confession of the sinner. Luther later remarked that "the condition was the cause of all calamity."[74] His instructor in the monastery sought to console him by pointing out that "God has commanded us to hope." This helped him to "believe somewhat in absolution" *(credere aliquantulum absolutionem)*. Nevertheless, he did not find true and lasting assurance of forgiveness, for he could not feel that his contrition and confession were what they should be. Thus the Catholic form of absolution actually bound the truly penitent sinner instead of freeing him, as Luther later observed.[76]

Luther, nevertheless, reaped some wholesome results from these struggles. His insight into the sinfulness and depravity of his nature was deepened, and he came to realize that sin does not lie primarily in the outward acts of man, but in the inclinations and desires of his heart.[77] His eyes were opened to see more clearly that in him, in his flesh, there was nothing good and that in the matter of his salvation he was entirely dependent upon the mercy of God.

In these conflicts and afflictions the counsel of Staupitz was like a "voice from heaven." Luther benefited greatly from the fivefold answer he received from Staupitz in regard to the problem of repentence.

1. Repentance begins with the love of God. This divine love, revealed in the sufferings and death of Christ, kindles a reciprocal love in the human heart, so that man begins to love the will of God and to hate sin. Thus is created in him a sincere sorrow over sin and true repentance, the source of which is the love of God for

man and not the love of man for God. The latter is an effect of the former.[78]

2. Contrition is a sorrow and anguish of the heart and conscience on account of sin and a desire to find mercy and pardon with God. No "work" of man can make him "worthy" of divine grace. The only way for sinful man to approach God is to admit his full guilt and unworthiness. Self-accusation and self-condemnation is the proper attitude of the penitent sinner before God.

3. Conviction of sin and the resultant anguish and self-accusation is the work of God, and not an accomplishment of man. Man cannot force it out of himself. Only the Law of God and the revelation of His love in Christ can bring it about in the human heart.

4. Since contrition cannot be considered a human achievement and merit, it is not necessary for man to examine his own heart in order to find a worthy contrition, which would qualify him for divine grace. Rather he should, being burdened with his sins, pay attention to the divine promise of pardon pronounced to him in absolution, firmly believing that in this assurance of forgiveness he has the pardon of God. The merits of Christ "cover" also the lack and weakness of contrition.

5. A complete enumeration of sins is not necessary in penance. Only actual sins against the Ten Commandments should be confessed. There would be no end to confession, if one attempted to confess all his sins. It is sufficient to confess those sins which one knows and which burden the conscience.[79] The significant importance of penance lies not in the confession, but in the absolution, through which God forgives sins.

---

[78] Theo. Dierks, "Luther's Spiritual Martyrdom and Its Appeasement," *Concordia Theological Monthly*, XII (1941), p. 107, says: "Staupitz did not and could not bring real peace to Luther, first, because he did not know that perfect contrition has its source in God's love to men — because God loves man, therefore man should love God and be sorry for his sins — and secondly, because he was a Catholic, laboring under the dictum: After baptism either satisfaction or punishment." — Exactly the opposite is true. Dierks is apparently totally ignorant of the true teaching of Staupitz.

[79] Some scholars (e. g., Boehmer, *op. cit.*, 109; Scheel, *op. cit* II, 376)

The doctrine of predestination was a further cause of much affliction and anguish of soul to Luther. His Nominalist teachers at Erfurt, following Gabriel Biel, taught that the salvation or perdition of man depends entirely upon the divine decree of predestination, which no man can change. On the other hand, however, they declared that the basis of election is the merit of man forseen from eternity *(propter meritum praevisum)*. By meriting the divine grace man merits his own election. This peculiar contradiction in the Nominalistic doctrine of election created in Luther an uncertainty which caused him to waver between hope and despair. Regardless of how he sought to merit grace and election, he could never attain certainty, since the final determining factor was the arbitrary decree of God. Whenever he experienced failure in his attempts to repent and find grace the thought arose in his mind that this was simply the result of the fact that God had not elected him and did not want to give him His grace.[80] The reaction was, as he pointed out later, that he was offended by the arbitrary predestination of God to the extent that he was tempted to hate and blaspheme God and to think of Him as an evil scoundrel.[81] Recognizing such thoughts as terrible sins, he was led into deeper despair.[82]

Staupitz held the Augustinian and not the Nominalistic view of predestination. Although his counsel to Luther ("it is better not to think of it [predestination], but to start from the wounds of Christ") seems to give the impression that he wanted Luther to

---

hold that Staupitz led Luther astray by turning his attention to gross outward sins and assuring him that he was not as great a sinner as he thought he was. This assertion, however, is fully refuted by the fact that Luther regarded this counsel of Staupitz helpful and passed it on to such as had an overscrupulous conscience and were troubled with insignificant matters. "Only sins which are generally acknowledged as mortal [should be confessed in penance], for if you confess all your sins, there would be no end to your confession" (WA. 2, 721, 24; cf. 7, 367, 30). — Bohlin, *op. cit.*, p. 36, is right in saying that Staupitz helped Luther to distinguish between real and imagined sins. So also Julius Koestlin, *Luthers Theologie* I (Stuttgart, 1901), p. 24.

give up the whole doctrine of predestination, such was not his real intention. This is evident also from the fact that Luther did not ignore predestination in his earliest lectures. By assisting Luther to a proper understanding of the doctrine of predestination, Staupitz provided him with a way of escape from the afflictions of his conscience relative to this doctrine. The new light Luther received was significant in a threefold sense.

1. Forseen merits are not the foundation and cause of election. Such is solely the undeserved mercy and love of God. Since salvation depends entirely upon the grace of God, man should not attempt by his own efforts and merits to prepare himself for grace. God does not elect man on the basis of his conduct and worthiness. The love of God toward sinners is revealed in the sacrifice of his Son and in the Sacraments. Man is to put his hope and trust in the "present predestination" revealed in the wounds of Christ and in the Gospel and not to meditate upon the hidden decree of God.

2. Anguish and terror of conscience is not a sign of reprobation, but of election, for they are the means by which God draws His elect to Christ. Also the anguish of heart which one experiences because of the temptation to blaspheme is a sign of election, since it shows that man is still in harmony with God and cannot consent to such thoughts. — The sufferings of Christ make it clear that the way to glory which God has ordained is the way of afflictions. Through patience in suffering the Christian is conformed to the image of Christ and shows himself a true follower of his Master. Also in this sense sufferings and afflictions are a sign of election.

3. We know the heart and will of God toward us through Christ. The divine love for sinners is revealed in the fact that God gave His only Son to be the propitiation for our sins. The dealings of God with men are determined by His fatherly love. Thus Staupitz gave Luther a new understanding of God and Christ: God is not a tyrant who deals with men in an arbitrary manner; Christ is not a fearful judge, but a merciful Savior. Whoever clings to Christ

and trusts in His atoning sacrifice and in the divine promises of grace will be saved.[83]

In short, Staupitz helped Luther to victory in his struggle with the doctrine of predestination by leading him not to discard the whole doctrine, but to understand it in a new way, so that it brought him comfort instead of affliction.

---

[83] Scheel, *op. cit.*, II, 377 ff., maintains that there was nothing new in the counsels of Staupitz concerning predestination. An "old brother" had reminded Luther of the words of the Creed: "I believe in the forgiveness of sins," encouraging him to hold to the revealed order of salvation. The Master of the Novices had said to him that his duty was to hope. Another Augustinian had advised him to seek predestination in the incarnate Christ whom God had given to men (TR. 3, 3,680). The reference to the wounds of Christ, Scheel says, was nothing especially evangelical or exceptional. Medieval Catholics often did the same.

True, there were evangelical tendencies in medieval Catholicism. The fact that, according to Luther's own testimony, the counsel of Staupitz was of particular significance to him was probably due to the fact that these evangelical tendencies were in a special sense centered in the person of Staupitz. He was the instrument whom God used to lead Luther from the bypaths of Nominalism and Semi-Pelagianism to an evangelical way of salvation.

Bohlin, *op. cit.*, p. 37, holds that Staupitz was unable to remove from Luther's heart the picture of Christ as a judge and legislator. To prove his point, Bohlin refers to the words of Luther in his larger *Commentary on Galatians:* "From boyhood on I was so imbued with the view [that Christ is a judge] that I became pale when I even heard the name of Christ, for I was persuaded that He is a judge" (40, I, 298, 29, Gal. 2:20). "For when we confessed most highly with our mouths that Christ had redeemed us from the tyranny and slavery of the Law, we felt in reality in our hearts, however, that He is a lawgiver, tyrant, judge, even more formidable than Moses himself" (*ibid.*, p. 562, 28, Gal. 4:4-5).

The truth is that as early as in his marginal notes on the *Sentences* of Lombard (which will be treated later) Luther speaks of Christ as the incarnate Savior of men. Accordingly, already then he was, to some extent at least, free from the idea that Christ is a formidable judge. His statement in the *Commentary on Galatians* simply means that at one time in his life he had such a conception. Furthermore, in the same commentary he complains that even in later life he was not wholly free from this idea, which had gone like oil into his bones (*ibid.*, p. 298, 26, Gal. 2:20).

Staupitz and Luther 33

Luther himself testifies to the fact that the most important practical significanc of Staupitz was that he led him to a personal faith in the forgiveness of sins in Christ. The chief difficulty of Luther had been his inability to believe that the remission proclaimed and offered in absolution truly belonged to him. A false conception of repentance and predestination stood in his way. Furthermore, he found it impossible to believe, because the conditional form of absolution based forgiveness in part on the contrition and satisfaction of the individual himself. Staupitz was instrumental in the clearing away of these stumbling blocks. Then he also absolved Luther of his sins in an evangelical manner, as may be gathered from the fact that Luther, according to his own words, received help from Staupitz in confession. With such a conception of the way of salvation as Staupitz had, it was not possible for him to pronounce absolution for the sake of the merits of Christ and the confession and satisfactions of the sinner himself. Luther was able at last to believe in the forgiveness of sins and to receive the blessings of the atoning sacrifice of Christ. For the first time he experienced the release of an evangelical confession and absolution and "ate the first fruits of the knowledge of and faith in Christ," as he later wrote.[84] The words "first fruits" show that up until then he had not possessed a personal knowledge of Christ and the Gospel through faith. The first rays of the sun of grace were cutting into the gray of dawn, but it would take a while longer before it would be shining in the glory of full daylight.

According to Luther's own testimony, Staupitz "started the doctrine" in regard to certain points, particularly repentance, atone-

---

[84] W. A. 54, 183. — Henry Strohl, *L'Evolution religieuse de Luther jusqu'a 1515* (Paris, 1922), pp. 120 ff., and E. Vogelsang, *Die Anfaenge von Luthers Christologie* (Berlin und Leipzig, 1929), pp. 90 f., give this matter an interpretation similar to that of Scheel. Strohl believes that the result of the counsels of Staupitz was only a "relative appeasement," not a real attaining of peace through the appropriation of the forgiveness of sins. About the same is the view of Philip S. Watson, *Let God be God* (London-Philadelphia, 1948), pp. 19 f.

ment, and predestination. Our investigation into the teachings of Staupitz and their significance to Luther has shown that this testimony is reliable.[85] It is true that Luther later received fuller light on these doctrines and saw more clearly the significance of Christ in the salvation of man, but the main features continued the same to the end of his life.[86]

The problem of Luther's discovery of the full evangelical insight into justification is distinct from his conversion or coming to a personal faith in Christ and receiving remission of sins in His blood. In the early phase of his development Luther was not troubled by the doctrine of justification. No mention is made of it in his references to the counsels and help he received from Staupitz. As we turn to this problem, which turned up later, we set ourselves the twofold task of seeking answers to the questions: first, What was the significance of Luther's discovery of the final Reformation insight into justification? and second, When did this discovery take place?

---

[85] Some scholars (e. g., Scheel and Boehmer) maintain that Luther exaggerated in his statements concerning the help he received from Staupitz. R. H. Fife, *Young Luther* (Grand Rapids, Mich., 1928), p. 142, is right in saying that it is no exaggeration on Luther's part, for others of his statements and facts concerning his development substantiate his story.

[86] Scheel, *op. cit.*, II, 378, asserts that since Luther does not teach predestination in his marginal notes to the *Sentences* of Lombard half a year after he had received Staupitz's counsels, he had not become a predestinarian in principle. — This statement is apparently a "lapse" in Scheel's thinking, for (1) he does not show — and nobody can — that Staupitz offered this help to Luther at a definite time in 1508—09 (Scheel himself points out that the two had intercourse also and more certainly in 1511—12 and (2) the marginal notes to the *Sentences* of Lombard make neither positive nor negative references in a definite way to the doctrine of predestination. — Luther's first treatment of the doctrine of predestination is to be found in his lectures on Romans, 1515—16, and then he was a predestinarian in principle. His brief reference to this doctrine in his lectures on the Psalms, 1513—15, seem to indicate that he was already then a predestinarian: Christ died only for the elect (WA. 4, 227). This statement reveals him as being then an extreme predestinarian, for this view he later rejected.

3

Luther's Discovery in the Tower

LUTHER'S OWN TESTIMONIES

IN the *Preface* to the Wittenberg edition of his works, which he wrote in 1545, Luther relates some of the most decisive events of his early life. Having discussed the first incidents in his struggle against indulgences, which began with posting the Ninety-Five Theses on October 31, 1517, Luther continued:

"And here you see in my own case how difficult it is to be freed from errors which have become established, constant usage, have become second nature. . . . At that time I had already for seven years read and taught the Holy Scriptures with great diligence both privately and publicly. I knew most of the Scriptures by heart and, furthermore, had eaten the first fruits of the knowledge of, and faith in, Christ, namely, that we are justified not by works, but by faith in Christ *(primitias cognitionis et fidei Christi hauseram, scilicet, non operibus, sed fide Christi nos iustos et salvos. fieri).* Finally — and of that I now speak — I already defended publicly the opinion that the Pope is not the head of the Church by divine right. . . ." [87]

Subsequently Luther writes of his negotiations with Karl von Miltitz (January, 1519), his disputation with Johann Eck at Leipzig (end of June and beginning of July, 1519), and the miserable death of Tetzel in the same year. He then goes on to say:

"Meanwhile, that same year I had again turned to the exposition of the Psalter, confident that after the academic treatment of the Epistles of St. Paul to the Romans and Galatians and the Epistle of the Hebrews I was better trained. Certainly I had been possessed by an unusually ardent desire to understand Paul in his Epistle to the Romans. Nevertheless, in spite of the ardor of my heart I was hindered by the unique word in the first chapter: 'The righteousness of God is revealed in it.' I hated that word 'righteousness of God,' because in accordance with the usage and custom of the doctors I had been taught to understand it philosophically as meaning, as they put it, the formal or active righteousness according to which God is righteous and punishes sinners and the unjust.

"As a monk I led an irreproachable life. Nevertheless I felt that I was a sinner before God. My conscience was restless, and I could not depend on God being propitiated by my satisfactions. Not only did I not love, but I actually hated the righteous God who punishes sinners. . . . Thus a furious battle raged within my perplexed conscience, but meanwhile I was knocking at the door of this particular Pauline passage, earnestly seeking to know the mind of the great Apostle.

"Day and night I tried to meditate upon the significance of these words: 'The righteousness of God is revealed in it, as it is written: The righteous shall live by faith.' Then, finally, God had mercy on me, and I began to understand that the righteousness of God is that gift of God by which a righteous man lives, namely, faith, and that this sentence: The righteousness of God is revealed in the Gospel, is passive, indicating that the merciful God justifies us by faith, as it is written: 'The righteous shall live by faith.' Now I felt as though I had been reborn altogether and had entered Paradise. In the same moment the face of the whole of Scripture became apparent to me. My mind ran through the Scriptures, as far as I was able to recollect them, seeking analogies in other phrases, such as the work of God, by which He makes us strong, the wisdom of God, by which He makes us wise, the strength of God, the salvation of God, the glory of God.

"Just as intensely as I had before hated the expression 'the righteousness of God,' I now lovingly praised this most pleasant word. This passage from Paul became to me the very gate to Paradise. Afterwards I read Augustine's treatise *On the Spirit and the Letter*, and, contrary to my expectation, I discovered a similar interpretation of the righteousness of God: that with which we are endued when God justifies us. Although up until now this had been imperfectly explained, and he does not clearly expound everything concerning imputation, he nevertheless seemed to teach the righteousness of God by which we are justified.

"Better equipped after these considerations, I began to interpret the Psalms the second time. The result would have been an extensive commentary, but I was again interrupted the following year by the summons of Emperor Charles V to the Diet at Worms." [88]

The *Table Talks* of Luther contain several accounts of his discovery of the true meaning of Rom. 1:17. Since they throw additional light upon the event, we shall quote the most important of them.

"These words 'righteous' and 'righteousness of God' *(iustus, iustitia Dei)* struck my conscience as flashes of lightning, frightening me each time I heard them: if God is righteous, He punishes. But by the grace of God, as I once meditated upon these words in this tower and *hypocaustum* (heated room): 'The righteous shall live by faith' and the 'righteousness of God,' there suddenly came into my mind the thought that if we as righteous are to live by faith, and if the righteousness of faith is to be for salvation to everyone who believes, then it is not our merit, but the mercy of God. Thus my soul was refreshed, for it is the righteousness of God by which we are justified and saved through Christ. These words became more pleasant to me. Through this word the Holy Spirit enlightened me in the tower." [89]

"At first whenever I read or sang the Psalm: 'Deliver me in Thy righteousness,' I was frightened, and I hated the words 'the righteousness of God' and 'the work of God,' for I believed that the righteousness of God meant His severe judgment. Was He to save me accordingly, I should be damned forever. But the words 'the mercy of God' and 'the help of God' I liked better. Thanks to God, when I understood the matter and learned that the righteousness of God means that righteousness by which He justifies us, the righteousness bestowed as a free gift in Jesus Christ, the grammar became clear and the Psalter more to my taste." [90]

"'For I am not ashamed of the Gospel . . . , for therein is revealed the righteousness of God' . . . I could not understand it otherwise than to mean the righteousness of God by which He Himself is righteous and judges righteously . . . , until I proceeded to read: 'The righteous shall live by his faith.' This sentence is the explanation of the righteousness of God. When I discovered this, I began to rejoice exceedingly. And so the way was clear when I read in the Psalms: 'Deliver me in Thy righteousness.' They revealed to me that the righteousness is the mercy of God by which He Himself justifies us by giving His grace." [91]

Even more significant than these statements is a story of Luther in which he relates the same event from a different point of view:

"I was astray for a long time. My inner condition was a mystery to me. True, I was aware of something, but what it was I did not know until I came to the passage in Romans 1: 'The righteous shall live by faith.' There I found help. Then I saw what Paul had in mind when He spoke of righteousness. There in the text stood 'righteousness.' I related the abstract and the concrete and became certain of my cause, learning to distinguish between the righteousness of the Law and the Gospel. Hitherto I lacked only a proper distinction between the Law and the Gospel. I considered both to be the same and Christ to differ from Moses only in time and perfection. It was when I discovered the difference between the Law and the Gospel, that they are two separate things, that I broke through." [92]

The Meaning of the Tower Discovery

Modern Luther research has made valiant efforts to solve the problem concerning the date of Luther's discovery in the tower. However, because of the fact that no earnest effort has ever been made to ascertain the meaning and content of this discovery, all attempts to determine its date have been seriously handicapped in their very beginning.[93] It has been usual to assume that with Luther it was simply a matter of whether the "righteousness of God" was His retributive justice, which considers the merits of man, or His grace, by which He makes righteous a man who in himself is a sinner.

But the problem is not as simple as that. Catholic Christianity contained elements which agreed, at least apparently, with the evangelical conception which Luther discovered. It is necessary to distinguish these elements from those that were new and characteristic of the evangelical insight of Luther.[94] True, at first glance it appears that the words of Luther himself suggest that it was merely a question involving the retributive and gracious righteousness of God. First impressions, however, are often misleading. Such was the case in regard to the words of Luther in reference to the help he received from Staupitz in his struggles with predestination. As was pointed out, Luther seems to suggest that Staupitz led him to give up altogether the doctrine of election. It also appears that Staupitz had nothing new to offer concerning repentance. But a closer investigation of the teachings of this friend and superior of Luther revealed that what first meets the eye is not the whole story. The same is true here. We cannot take the words superficially as they appear to us, but must seek to know what Luther actually meant.

Our first concern is to determine how the passage Rom. 1:17 was commonly explained prior to the discovery that Luther made.

It is an established fact that the teachers of the Church interpreted this statement of Paul to mean not the "active" justice of God by which He punishes the sinners and the unjust, but, as

Augustine explained it, the grace which God bestows upon man and by which He makes him righteous.⁹⁵

Ambrosiaster, who, along with Augustine, was one of the most influential exegetes of the Church, explained this passage to mean that God mercifully receives those who flee to Him for refuge, because He is righteous in keeping His promises.⁹⁶

The prevailing exegesis combined these interpretations in one way or another.⁹⁷

We may safely assume that Luther already early in his life was familiar with this interpretation.⁹⁸ He presents this Augustinian view in all his writings that date from the very earliest period of his life.⁹⁸ᵃ

---

⁹⁷ In 1905 the Roman Catholic H. Denifle published an extensive study, *Luther und Luthertum. Ergaenzungen. I. Quellenbelege. Die abendlaendischen Schriftausleger ueber iustitia Dei (Rom. 1, 17) und iustificatio,* on the question whether or not the teachers of the Church explained the words *iustitia Dei* in Rom. 1:17 to mean His punishing justice. He showed that out of "60 teachers of the Latin Church" all interpreted these words as meaning "the righteousness through which we become righteous, God's undeserved justifying grace, the real justification of men received through faith" (*op. cit.,* 2d ed., p. 395).

Karl Holl restudied the problem and presented his results in an article "Die iustitia Dei in der vorlutherischen Bibelauslegung des Abendlandes," *Festgabe zu A. von Harnack* (1921), pp. 73—92 (the same in Holl, *Gesammelte Aufsaetze* III, pp. 177—181). Although Holl criticized Denifle on certain points, he acknowledged Denifle to be in the right on the main points in regard to the exegesis of the Western Church. Our presentation is based on this article of Holl.

⁹⁸ Fr. Loofs, *Leitfaden zum Studium der Dogmengeschichte* (Halle, 1906), p. 689, says that Luther knew this interpretation as early as before his journey to Rome (1510—11). It is to be found in his marginal notes to the *Sentences* of Lombard. It was also one of the leading ideas of Augustine's *On the Spirit and the Letter,* to which he referred several times in these notes. So also Adolf Hamel, *Der junge Luther und Augustin I* (Guetersloh, 1934), pp. 10 f., and A. Hardeland, "Der Begriff der iustitia passiva bei Luther," *Christentum und Wissenschaft* (1926), p. 63.

⁹⁸ᵃ This proposition will be substantiated by our study further on.

What conclusions are we to draw from this fact? Are we to conclude, as some scholars do, that Luther made a mistake? Before resorting to such an emergency explanation, let us seek other possible solutions. Actually, we believe, the key for the right interpretation of his discovery in the tower is the very fact that already early in his life Luther was acquainted with the explanation that the "righteousness of God" in Rom. 1:17 means the righteousness by which God makes man righteous.

When Luther in 1545 gave the "great testimony" of his development, he had for a long time already possessed his evangelical insight into justification. The Augustinian conception of justification as a gradual healing process with the non-imputation of sins as a supplement did not meet with his approval. Luther then taught that man is righteous in the sight of God, not because he has become, or started to become, such, but because Christ has fulfilled the Law for him, and God imputes the "good works" of Christ to him as his righteousness. Renewal is an effect or fruit of justifying faith. Luther regarded it a dangerous error to identify justification with renewal, or faith with its fruits. As he saw it, such a doctrine robs man of peace of conscience, casting him back on a secret self-righteousness or an "active" work-righteousness.

Is it even reasonable to think that toward the end of his life as a reformer Luther wanted to describe the "discovery" of the Augustinian-Catholic doctrine of justification as the most decisive event in his development, a doctrine that he then regarded as false? Can we assume that Luther was not able to differentiate between his own doctrine of justification and that of the Roman Church? Must we assume that he considered it an important discovery when he "found" the doctrine of the Catholics?

It is hardly possible to think of anything more foolish and senseless, and yet that is exactly what most of the Luther scholars of our day contend. They maintain that the "tower experience" of Luther was simply the discovery of the interpretation which was the common property of almost all of the teachers of the Church. One finds it difficult to believe that such a view could be the "result" of "scientific" Luther research.[99] Only one interpretation is possible, namely, that in these testimonies of his own development, Luther intended to say that in his "tower experience" he discovered the reformation insight into justification. Thus he was equipped to expound the Scriptures in the evangelical manner.

But do the words of Luther lend themselves to such an interpretation?

Luther says:

"Then I began to understand the righteousness of God to be that by which a righteous man lives through the gift of God, namely, by faith, and that the sentence 'the righteousness of God is revealed through the Gospel,' is passive. Thereby the merciful God justifies us by faith, as it is written: The righteous shall live by faith."

The words "gift of God" and "passive righteousness" naturally mean, in the mouth of old Luther, the alien, donated, and imputed righteousness of Christ of which he spoke so often, particularly in his *Commentary on Galatians*. This is evident also from his *Table Talks* in which he states that the righteousness of which Paul speaks in Rom. 1:17 "is not our merit, but the mercy of God . . . by which we are justified and saved through Christ." It is "that righteousness by which He justifies us through the righteousness presented to us as a free gift in Jesus Christ," "the mercy (*misericordia*) of God by which He Himself justifies us by giving us His grace."

---

[99] R. H. Fife, *op. cit.*, pp. 163 f., is honest and open about expressing the view that is prevalent among many Lutheran scholars today. He says that Luther's "discovery" in the Wittenberg monastery was no real discovery at all. Many scholars of the Middle Ages, Gabriel Biel excepted, possessed that truth. For Luther himself it was a discovery, but not for the theological world in general. — Such a statement on the part of Fife may sound surprising and strange, but actually it expresses the opinion of most Luther scholars.

One comes to the same conclusion from the statement of Luther that his discovery in the tower opened his eyes to see the proper distinction between the Law and the Gospel. This is the distinction found in his mature teachings. The Augustinian-Catholic doctrine was a confusion of the Law and the Gospel. According to it "Christ differed from Moses only in time and perfection."

It is impossible to explain these statements as referring to the Augustinian interpretation, that God justifies the sinner by creating in him a new will, so that he begins to fulfill the Law. At the time when Luther uttered the statements under consideration he regarded this Augustinian view as false.

Our conclusions receive further confirmation when we consider the words of Luther concerning Augustine. He says: "Although . . . he does not clearly expound everything concerning imputation, he nevertheless seems to teach the righteousness of God by which we are justified." According to these words the crucial point in the discovery of Luther was the doctrine of the imputation of righteousness. From the point of view of Luther it was at this very point that the teaching of Augustine lacked clearness. And it was this that Luther previously had not understood. True, he had known something of imputation, namely, as Augustine interpreted it; but now he saw this doctrine in its Scriptural light: we are justified by the imputed righteousness of Christ.

As a result of this discovery Luther was overjoyed to the point that he felt he had entered Paradise. Now he realized that it was unnecessary for him to look to his renewal and his progress in holiness for his justification before God. He could rest with confidence on the finished work and righteousness of Christ.

Prior to this discovery Luther had been in the bonds of a secret "active" righteousness. He was under the impression that man must become "actively" righteous in order to stand before God, who judges him according to the character of his person and behavior.[100] It is true that according to the Augustinian-Catholic doctrine this new quality in man is the work of divine grace. The more serious and sincere people, however, could not but anxiously consider the progress in holiness in themselves and judge according to it whether there was for them any hope of inheriting eternal life. If they found that there was some real progress in their sanctification, they were assured of their salvation. But then they had actually already fallen into the pit of self-righteousness. On the other hand, if they discovered no such growth in holiness, they despaired of their salvation. E. Vogelsang is right in saying that "even when Augustine called it [the righteousness of God] a righteousness which is given to us as a gift, it kindled the deepest afflictions in the heart of Luther, because he did not find this donated real righteousness and goodness *(reale Recht- und Gutsein)* in himself." [101]

As long as Luther was under the impression that the righteousness which God requires of man is his "active" goodness and innocence of obedience and love, produced by the infused grace, and

---

[100] Luther's teaching of the "passive righteousness of God" has been treated by several Luther scholars. Loofs in 1911 ("Justitia Dei passiva in Luther Anfaengen," *Theologische Studien und Kritiken*, pp. 461 ff.) showed that in his early life Luther understood this term differently. In his early writings it means that man acknowledges that God is right in His judgment of him. By confessing his sinfulness and condemning himself man "justifies God." In later life, in his mature period, Luther understood by this term the imputed righteousness. — O Scheel, "Die justitia passiva in Luthers reformatorischer Rechtfertigungslehre," *Festschrift zum 70. Geburtstage von Theodor Brieger*, 1912, p. 93 ff., criticized certain statements of Loofs. The latter answered in his essay "Der articulus stantis et cadentis ecclesiae," 1917. Scheel took up the question again in his *Martin Luther* II, 589 f. A. Hardeland treats the matter in his *op. cit.* (1926).

[101] E. Vogelsang, *Die Anfaenge von Luthers Christologie* (Berlin und Leipzig, 1929), pp. 47 f. — Strangely enough, Vogelsang does not make use of this fine insight in his interpretation of the discovery of Luther. He explains it in the usual way: Luther found the Augustinian conception. Holl, "Die justitia Dei passiva . . .", *op. cit.*, p. 91, comes to a similar conclusion.

Luther's Discovery in the Tower

that He judges man according to his actual condition, it was impossible for him to have true and lasting peace in his heart. The deeper his knowledge and conviction of his sinfulness was, the more painful was the anguish caused by the Augustinian conception of justification. To be sure, Staupitz had helped him to believe in the forgiveness of sins in Christ. But he did not realize that thereby he was also justified before God. He was unable to identify the forgiveness of sins and justification. Consequently he could not consider himself as yet righteous in the sight of God. At best it was an insignificant beginning of righteousness. This lack of understanding partly destroyed the peace which he had found through faith in the forgiveness of sins.

The result of these inner struggles was the discovery of the truth that God justifies the sinner by declaring him righteous for Christ's sake without his own merit and worthiness. God adopts the sinner as His child on the basis of the merits of Christ alone.

In one of the table talks to which reference has already been made Luther says that he made no distinction between Moses and Christ except as to time and perfection. He thought that the Gospel makes it possible for us to fulfill the Law and so to become righteous before God. Now he understood that Christ had fulfilled the Law for us, and that we are justified when God imputes to us this perfect fulfillment of Christ.

Luther makes the statement in his *Preface* of 1545 that already before his discovery of the true meaning of Rom. 1:17 and Ps. 31:2 he had "eaten the first fruits of the knowledge of and faith in Christ, namely, that we are justified and saved not through works, but through faith in Christ." But the word "the righteousness of God" *(iustitia Dei)* continued to confuse and trouble him. In one of his table talks (which dates from 1542 or 1543) he expresses the same fact. "I knew something, but I did not know, nevertheless, what it was until I came to the passage in Romans 1: 'The righteous shall live by faith.' That helped me. Then I saw what Paul meant when he spoke of righteousness." Prior to this discovery Luther "lacked nothing" except an understanding of the true distinction between the Law and the Gospel. The words of Paul in Rom. 1:17 became the key to such an understanding, and he "broke through."

In the light of the above statements, the "tower experience" of Luther was not the beginning, but the relative end of his development. Prior to that he knew, in the Augustinian sense, that man is justified and saved through faith in Christ and not by works. It was the discovery of the true meaning of Rom. 1:17 that opened to him the final evangelical insight into justification.

To summarize the results of our study:

1. The "tower experience" of Luther was his discovery of the full Reformation insight into justification, that God justifies the sinner by graciously imputing, or reckoning, the merits of Christ to him as his righteousness. Justification is not a change in man, but the gracious declaration of God by which He pronounces righteous the sinner who in himself is not righteous.

2. From another point of view, the content of the discovery was the "Lutheran" distinction between the Law and the Gospel.

3. Luther's experience in the tower was not his conversion. It was the final exegetico-religious discovery of the evangelical way of salvation. We say exegetico-religious, because it was not simply an exegetical discovery of the true teaching of Scripture on this point; neither was it a mere subjective personal experience. At the same time that it was the discovery of the true interpretation of Scripture, it was also an answer to a deep personal spiritual yearning, which resulted in the attainment of a deeper personal assurance of salvation or justification.[102]

---

[102] Some time ago there was a strong tendency in Luther research to regard the "tower experience" as the "conversion" of Luther (so, e. g., Scheel, *op. cit.*). J. Mackinnon, *Luther and the Reformation,* I (London, 1925), p. 329, writes: "The genesis of Lutheran Reformation is undoubtedly to be

Luther's Discovery in the Tower

We now have a standard or criterion for the evaluation of the teachings of Luther on justification and sanctification in his early period.[103] Our next task is to study the early lectures and writings

---

sought in the sphere of religious experience rather than in that of theological speculation."

J. von Walter, "Der Abschluss der Entwicklung des jungen Luther," *Zeitschrift fuer systematische Theologie* (1923), expressed the view that Luther came to faith through the help of Staupitz and that his discovery in the tower was a Scriptural-theologico-scientific confirmation of the faith he already possessed. — There is much truth in what v. Walter states, although his interpretation errs on certain points.

The past two decades have witnessed a reaction against this tendency to identify the "conversion" and "tower experience" of Luther. Some scholars have expressed themselves in favor of the view of v. Walter. So, e. g., E. Wolf, "Ueber neuere Lutherliteratur und den Gang der Lutherforschung," *Christentum und Wissenschaft* (1933), pp. 225 f. Anders Nygren, "Raamattu ja saarna" (Scripture and the Sermon), *Vartija* (Helsinki, 1946) p. 65, says very aptly: ". . . the Reformation . . . was not born through subjective practice of piety, but through meditation upon the objective meaning of the Word. No one has delved as deep as Luther into the literal sense of Scripture itself, . . . and his efforts to clarify the objective content of the Word was crowned by the rediscovery of the forgotten Gospel."

[103] Em. Hirsch, "Initium theologiae Lutheri," *Festgabe fuer Julius Kaftan* (Tuebingen, 1920), pp. 165 ff., used the following as his criteria in his evaluation of the early teachings of Luther: (1) the "righteousness of God" is not a retributory, but a donated righteousness; (2) it is the righteousness of faith; (3) it is righteousness before God, not men (Watson, *op. cit.*, pp. 20 f., uses about the same criteria).

These criteria contain common Christian elements which even the Roman Catholics accept, with an interpretation somewhat different from that of the Lutherans. An estimation of the early teaching of Luther according to such criteria leads necessarily to wrong results.

The same is true of the criterion of Alfred Kurz, *Die Heilsgewissheit bei Luther* (Guetersloh, 1933), pp. 262 f.: The certainty of salvation in a threefold sense: certainty of faith, justification, and sanctification. This criterion has only *one* element which is characteristic of the evangelical faith and the theology of Luther.

The only adequate criterion for the estimation of the early teachings of

of the Reformer with the purpose of determining when the new insight first appears.[104] After that it will be a rather simple matter to solve the problem of the date of Luther's "tower experience." [105]

Luther is the *content*, or nature, of Luther's mature doctrine of justification and sanctification, with the characteristic features which distinguish it from the Augustinian-Catholic conception.

[104] With regard to the *place* of his discovery Luther says in a table talk (TR. 2, 1681): "The Holy Spirit has revealed to me this art in this Cl" (Diese kunst hat mir der Spiritus Sanctus auf das Cl eingegeben). Grisar explains that the abbreviation "Cl" means *cloaca* (toilet, privy). This interpretation is impossible for the simple reason that the pronoun "das" is *neuter*, while the noun "*cloaca*" is feminine. The noun "claustrum" is neuter. It is natural that Luther wanted to say that his discovery took place "in this claustrum" (monastery). We cannot imagine him making a grammatical blunder and using a neuter pronoun with a feminine noun. — In another of his table talks Luther says that the discovery took place in a "*hypocaustum*," or heated room, of the monastery. When he became professor, he was given a heated room for his study. There he was studying the Scriptures when his eyes were opened to see the truth.

[105] Luther scholars have proposed several solutions for the problem of the date of the "tower experience." They may be grouped as follows:

1. *Luther's discovery took place while he was preparing his first lectures on the Psalms, between the late fall of 1512 and the summer of 1513.* So, e. g., H. Boehmer, *Luthers erste Vorlesung* (Leipzig, 1924), pp. 37, 52, and *Der junge Luther* (Gotha, 1925), pp. 110 ff.; Fr. Loofs, "Luthers Rechtfertigungslehre," *Mitteilungen der Luther-Gesellschaft*, 1924, p. 84; H. Wendorf, "Der Durchbruch der neuen Erkenntnis Luthers im Lichte der handschriftlichen Ueberlieferung," *Historische Vierteljahrschrift*, 1932, pp. 315 f.; A. Hamel *op. cit.*, I, p. 197; J. Mackinnon, *op. cit.*, I, p. 151.

2. *The "tower experience" took place during Luther's first lectures on the Psalms, 1513–14.* So, e. g., E. Hirsch, *op. cit.*, p. 161 (the new conception appears for the first time in the explanation of Psalms 31/32); J. v. Walter, *op. cit.*, pp. 424 f. (accepts the results of Hirsch); E. Vogelsang, *op. cit.*, pp. 4, 10, 59, 81 (the first clear expression of the new conception is to be found in the explanation of Psalms 71/72); M. Reu, *Luther's German Bible* (Columbus, Ohio, 1934), pp. 106, 136 (accepts the results of Vogelsang); Fife, *op. cit.*, pp. 179 f. (during the first lectures on the Psalms); Eino Sormunen, *Jumalan armo* II (Helsinki, 1934), p. 47, and *Kerjäläisiä me olemme* (Helsinki, 1947), p. 60, (during the first lectures on the Psalms 1513–14); L.

Pinomaa, "Lutherin reformatoorisen murroksen ajankohta" (The Date of Luther's Reformation Crisis), *Teologinen Aikakauskirja*, No. 1, 1941 (Helsinki), and *Der existenzielle Charakter der Theologie Luthers* (Helsinki, 1940), pp. 131 ff. (the results of both Boehmer and Vogelsang are correct in their own ways); Philip S. Watson, *op. cit.*, p. 28 (accepts Hirsch's and Vogelsang's position); Gordon Rupp, *Luther's Progress to the Diet of Worms, 1521* (London, 1951), p. 38 (during the lectures on the Psalms, 1513–14); E. G. Schwiebert, *Luther and His Times* (St. Louis, Mo., 1951), p. 288 (when he was working on the 71st Psalm, some time in the fall of 1514).

3. *Luther's discovery occurred sometime during the years 1514–16.* So, e. g., Preserved Smith, "A Decade of Luther Study," *Harvard Theological Review*, 1921, p. 112 ("when Luther had begun to lecture on Romans, in the late spring or early summer of 1515"); in his earlier work, *The Life and Letters of Martin Luther* (Boston, Mass., 1911), p. 23, Smith stated that it took place sometime before 1515; A. Kurz, *op. cit.*, pp. 180 f., (soon after the end of Luther's lectures on Romans, in the autumn of 1516); A. V. Mueller, *op. cit.*, pp. 122, 136 (at the end of 1514, while preparing his lectures on Romans); H. J. Iwand, *op. cit.*, p. 33 (after a lengthy period of academic teaching).

4. *Luther is right in stating that his "tower experience" took place toward the end of 1518.* So, e. g., Th. Harnack, *Luthers Theologie* I, pp. 8, 34, and H. Grisar, *Martin Luthers Leben und sein Werk* (Freiburg im Breisgau. 1926), p. 97.

PART TWO

Luther's Early Conception of Justification and His Final Discovery of the Gospel

4

The Marginal Notes on Augustine and Lombard and the Decisive Influence of Staupitz

THE marginal notes that Luther made to Augustine's books in 1509 and to the *Sentences* of Lombard in 1509–11 bear out the fact that he was then a faltering follower of the Nominalists. The influence of Augustine and Staupitz had begun to wean him away from this theology, but no definite break had occurred as yet.

In his notes to Augustine's writing *On the Trinity* Luther states: "What He (*sc.*, Christ) says elsewhere, 'I am the Resurrection and the Life,' may be correctly explained to refer to His deity, but, more properly understood, it means His humanity, at least in the context in which He continues to state: 'Who believes in Me.' For this 'to believe' implies faith in His humanity, which is given us for life and salvation here and now, for He Himself is our life, our righteousness, and our resurrection. He says that He will give Himself to us for eternal life. . . . Thus it seems that in that passage He speaks of the life and resurrection through faith in Him. But that is . . . in His humanity. After this life follows eternal life." [106]

These words express simple truths of Scripture and are also in harmony with the teachings of Augustine and Staupitz. The statement is too brief, however, to afford making any important inferences from them. It is quite possible, however, that the influence of Staupitz is evident in the emphasis upon the humanity of Christ and redemption through His death.

The marginal notes that Luther made to the *Sentences* of Lombard are more extensive and therefore provide a more adequate picture of his thinking during that period of his life. In one of his notes he says:

". . . love is always given with the Holy Spirit, and the Holy Spirit with love. . . . The Master [Lombard] does not speak at all absurdly when he says that the *habitus* is the Holy Spirit. . . . Otherwise it may be said. . . . that the Holy Spirit is the love *(caritas)* which is united with the will for the purpose of producing the act of loving." [107]

These thoughts expressed here also were characteristic of the teaching of Staupitz. They indicate, very possibly, that his counsel was already bearing fruit in the mind of Luther.

The Occamistic theology, which had a dominating influence in Erfurt, laid strong emphasis upon the truth that Christianity rests on the revelation of God. Scripture is the highest, in fact the only source of Christian truth, and it is also the supreme standard and rule of Christian doctrine.[108] This teaching of the Occamists appears to have had a significant influence on the development of Luther, as is evident from his words to his Occamist teacher Trutvetter: "You were the first from whom I learned that we must believe only the canonical books; everything else is to be judged, as Augustine, yea, and even Paul and John teach." [109]

This principle Luther expressed beautifully in his marginal notes to Lombard:

"Arguments based on reason determine nothing, but because Holy Scripture says that it is true, it is true." [110]

"Although famous doctors hold this opinion, they do not have Scripture on their side, but only arguments of reason; but I have Scripture on my side . . . and so I say with the Apostle: 'Though an angel of heaven, that is, a doctor of the Church, teach otherwise, let him be anathema.'" [111]

Luther availed himself of this argument against some of the teachers of Scholasticism, but not as yet against the Church as such. However, there is evident in his words something of that courageous clinging to the words of Scripture which enabled him to break the bonds of time-honored and almost universal tradition and to return to the Gospel of the Scriptures. Such a development was not possible without many bitter inner struggles, as he pointed out in his *Preface* of 1545 and elsewhere.[112]

The marginal notes to Lombard also bear traces of Luther's struggle for deliverance from the shackles of Nominalism. God's justice is identical with His will, he writes, and God's will is always good.[113] Salvation is entirely the work of God. It depends not on our efforts and abilities, but on the mercy of God.[114] With the powers that we possess by nature we cannot change our will or accomplish anything toward our salvation. Co-operation with the divine will is possible only if our will is restored by divine grace.[115] Thoughts such as these are in full agreement with the teachings of Augustine and Staupitz.

Luther follows Augustine and the Catholic doctrine also in stressing that we are justified by faith which works through love.[116] But whatever we may have in the way of merits is the result of grace. God crowns only His own works in us.[117]

Rom. 1:17 is discussed only once in the marginal notes to Lombard. Luther does not, however, make mention of the righteousness of God (*iustitia Dei*). He pays attention only to the words "from faith to faith." In agreement with the interpretation of Augustine he explains these words to mean "from the faith of a believer to the faith of another."

It is apparent that under the influence of Augustine and Staupitz, Luther's development in the direction of an evangelical understanding had begun already in 1509—11. In his theology he is closer to Augustine and Paul than to Occam and Biel.[118] He knows something of the utter sinfulness and helplessness of man and of his dependence upon the grace of God. Later Luther remarks that Lombard was a "good man" who taught that the free will of man can do only evil.[119]

In a letter dated March 17, 1509 (Enders 1, 5), Luther speaks humbly and trustfully of reliance on the grace of God and on His gentle guidance. He praises that theology which lifts man above his natural righteousness and offers nourishment to the yearning soul. This letter may be an indication of the fact that the source of unrest in the soul of Luther had been removed to a certain extent — unless the time of the writing of this letter was simply one of those peaceful periods of his life, which were never entirely lacking. At any rate, it is impossible to draw any definite conclusions from this letter in regard to the spiritual state of Luther at that time.

Luther associated with Staupitz in Wittenberg in the winter of 1508—09 and from 1511 to the fall of 1512.[120] After Luther returned from Rome in 1512, Staupitz urged him to begin working for the degree of Doctor of Theology. Luther, however, was unwilling. His reasons and excuses to his superior reveal a rather despondent state of soul.[121]

On May 21, 1537, Luther delivered a sermon (WA. 5, 86) which contains some important information regarding the time of the decisive help of Staupitz. He says that when he became a doctor (which took place on October 19, 1512), he did not know the light. Most Luther scholars understand these words to refer to Luther's discovery of the evangelical insight into justification. Such an assumption, however, receives no support from the facts. In this sermon Luther does not speak of justification at all, but of those problems in regard to which he received help from Staupitz. His words are these:

"We have attained light again. But at the time I became a doctor, I did not know. . . . God did not send His Son to judge. Therefore we cannot see Christ and the heart of God in that way."

Luther further declares that the heart and grace of God are to be seen only in Christ. In Him God has revealed His will to us.

Outside of Christ, God is unknown to us. It is through Him that the love of God shines forth. All of these truths Luther learned from Staupitz, and they were known to him prior to his "tower experience." It was at these very points that Staupitz, as Luther himself says, "started the doctrine."

Both in his statements concerning the help he received from Staupitz and in this sermon Luther speaks of light. At the time he received his doctorate he did not possess the light, but the light of the Gospel began to shine into his heart through the message proclaimed by Staupitz. Since in both instances the context of ideas is identical, it is only natural to infer that Luther is speaking of the same incident, namely, the receiving of faith in the forgiveness of sins and grace in Christ. This took place in connection with his confession to Staupitz, through the counsels and absolution he received from him.

There is yet another fact that throws light on the problem of the time when Luther received from Staupitz the help which proved so decisive. The journey which Luther made to Rome in 1510—11 was an outcome of dissension between the reformed and unreformed Augustinian convents. Some of the German Augustinians opposed the reforms attempted by Staupitz. Among the convents that resented such efforts was the monastery of Erfurt. Luther was one of the delegates sent to present their case in the court of the Pope. It was not until after his return from Rome that Luther changed his mind and joined the party supporting Staupitz. One cannot conceive of Luther's going to Rome to work against Staupitz after having received such invaluable aid from him in his spiritual struggle.[122]

The "shining of the light of the Gospel" into the heart of Luther

---

[122] Wolf, *op. cit.*, p. 250, assumes that the decisive help of Staupitz had been received prior to Luther's journey to Rome. We cannot agree with this view. The marginal notes of 1509—11 give no indisputable evidence on the matter. It is possible that Luther received some help before his journey, but the decisive event occurred after his promotion to doctor.

transpired after he received his doctorate on October 19, 1512, as is evident from his statement in the sermon referred to above. Possibly it occurred soon afterwards, for that autumn was the last time Luther and Staupitz had opportunity for mutual intercourse. The following summer (1513) Luther entered upon his first lecture course on the Psalms.[123] The contents of these lectures, as will be pointed out in the next chapter, show that the decisive step had already been taken.

---

[123] On the date of the beginning of these lectures, see, e. g., Boehmer, *Luthers erste Vorlesung*, pp. 8 f., and Hamel, *op. cit.*, I, 26. — Luther used the Vulgate (the Latin translation of the Bible, done by Jerome ca. A. D. 400), in which the numbering of the Psalms, beginning with Psalm 10, differs from ours (which is in accordance with the Hebrew text). E. g., our Psalm 31 corresponds to Psalm 30 in the Vulgate. We indicate by "Ps. 30/31."

5

Luther's First Lectures on the Psalms, 1513—1515

LUTHER started his first course of lectures on the Psalms in 1513, probably in the summer, and continued them to October, 1515.[124]

---

[124] In his letter to Spalatin in 1515 (Enders 1, 26) Luther states that he was at work preparing for publication his lectures on the Psalms. From this A. V. Mueller, *op. cit.*, pp. 128 ff., concludes that Luther then altered the entire manuscript and that in its present form it contains but little from the year 1513.

Em. Hirsch studied the manuscript in a photographic reproduction and published his results in his article *Initium theologiae Lutheri* (1920). He sought to determine to what extent Luther had altered them and came to the conclusion that most of the lectures are unaltered. Some changes are to be found only in the *scholia* (*glossa* is a brief interpretation of the text, *scholium*, plural *scholia*, a more extended exposition of its thought) of Psalm 1.

H. Boehmer studied the original manuscript a little later, publishing his results in the work *Luthers erste Vorlesung* (1924). He maintained that only Sheets 2—5 in the *scholia* of Psalm 1 (WA. 3, 15—26, 18) and Sheets 18—25 of Psalm 4 (WA. 3, 39—60, 7) belong to the altered portion. The rest of the commentary consists of the original lecture notes (p. 37).

E. Vogelsang made a restudy of the manuscript, presenting the results in his work *Die Anfaenge von Luthers Christologie* (1929). In the main he accepted the results of Hirsch as to the textual criticism of these lectures. Disregarding parts of the *scholia* of Psalms 1 and 4, we have the original lectures in WA. (pp. 41, 59, 87).

H. Wendorf studied the manuscript again a few years later and published his findings in the article "Der Durchbruch der neuen Erkenntnis Luthers

In the time of Luther a lecturer on Biblical exegesis was required to present to his students the thoughts of approved expositors. This was demanded also of Luther. He relied particularly on Augustine's commentary on the Psalms,[125] Lyra's commentary, and the most modern work of his time, LeFevre d'Etaples' (Faber Stapulensis') *Psalterium quintuplex* (1509). However, beginning with Psalms 90, quotations are fewer. Luther gives his own explanations.

According to the exegetical rules of his day, Luther was necessitated to discover a fourfold meaning *(Quadriga)* in the text:

Literal: Christ. — E. g., in Ps. 31:1 the words "Deliver me in Thy righteousness" are a prayer of Christ.

Allegorical: The Church, the communion of saints. In Ps. 30/31:2 Christ prays in and for the members of His body as its head.

Tropological: The individual believer. Ps. 30/31:2 is also his prayer.

Anagogical: The eschatological sense. Ps. 30/31:2 refers also to the final salvation in the Kingdom of Glory.[126]

---

im Lichte der handschriftlichen Ueberlieferung" (1932). He held that Boehmer was correct in most cases. The WA. text of these lectures is reliable. If we set aside WA. 3, 15—26, 8 and 3, 39—60, 7, we have the original notes of Luther (pp. 278, 302).

In regard to the text of these lectures these scholars are unanimous on the main point, namely, that with the exception of some parts of the *scholia* of Psalms 1 and 4 the WA. text of these lectures is a reliable source for an understanding of Luther's views at this time. Opinions differ only on the question when Luther's new insight into justification makes its first appearance in these lectures.

[126] E. von Dobschuetz, "Vom vierfachen Schriftsinn," *Harnack-Ehrung* (1921), pp. 1 ff., gives an account of the history of this method. Fritz Hahn, "Luthers Auslegungsgrundsaetze und ihre theologischen Voraussetzungen," *Zeitschrift fuer systematische Theologie*, 1934, shows how Luther used this method. — Luther said later: "The monks and scholastic teachers . . . have the tradition that Scripture contains a fourfold meaning: literal, tropological, allegorical, and anagogical, and according to these they interpreted inaptly almost all the words of the Bible. So Jerusalem means literally the city that

Luther's First Lectures on the Psalms

In his lectures on the Psalms Luther contrasts *spirit* and *letter* in the text of the Bible. Such a contrast originates in the Biblical distinction between prophecy and fulfillment or "shadow" and "reality." But the influence of the Neo-Platonic contrast between the visible and invisible, the sensible and the intelligible, the *Abbild* (earthly things) and *Urbild* (archetype, pattern, heavenly things) is also noticeable in this differentiation. All created things are parables or symbols of heavenly things and thus contain hidden teachings.[127] This Neo-Platonic coloring in the lectures of Luther had its source especially in Augustine and Faber Stapulensis.[128]

From the point of view of the doctrine of justification the tropological or moral sense of Scripture is most important. According to it the Scriptural statements concerning Christ (His words, deeds, and sufferings) pertain also to those who are His own. As Christ humbled Himself and entered glory through shame, suffering, and death, His own also must walk this same way in the footsteps of their Master.

The central thought of the tropological interpretation, that God deals with His children in the same manner as He dealt with Christ, is inseparably connected with the doctrine of justification throughout these lectures. Christ is the pattern (exemplar, Urbild,

---

has that name, tropologically the clean conscience, allegorically the struggling Church, and anagogically the heavenly fatherland of triumphant Church" (40, 1, 663, 13, *Commentary on Galatians*, 4:26).

[127] *Ibid.*, pp. 173 f. — At this time Luther did not distinguish between Scriptural Christianity and Neo-Platonic mysticism. He praised the negative theology of Areopagite as "most perfect." H. Quiring, "Luther und die Mystik," *Zeitschrift fuer systematische Theologie*, 1936, p. 162.

[128] A. Hamel, *op. cit.* I, p. 224, asserts that the Augustinian Neo-Platonism appears but "sporadically" in these lectures and that Luther received from Augustine religious rather than philosophical influences. — Neo-Platonism was primarily a religio-philosophical doctrine of the way of salvation. Even its philosophical ideas were religious through and through. Augustine's teaching of the way of salvation was a synthesis of Christian and Neo-Platonic ideas, the divergence of which he did not see. It is not possible, therefore, to make such a distinction between his religious and philosophical ideas as Hamel does.

archetype) of the way of salvation. God justifies man by curing and cleansing him from sin. This He accomplishes through humility, mortification of the flesh, and resurrection to a new life.[129]

He who desires to be justified by God must give up all self-assertion and self-defense. The man who is truly humble is beautiful and righteous in God's sight, for he admits that God is right in judging him and acknowledges that God is the only righteous one, confessing his own sins and accusing and condemning himself.[130]

"Not he who thinks he is humble, but he who regards himself as detestable and damnable, blaming and condemning his sins, is righteous.[131]

By confessing his sinfulness and by accusing and condemning himself, man honors and "justifies" God, for thereby he admits that the divine judgment in His Word is just. In so doing man is at one with God, thinking and saying of himself the same as God says of him. Such a man is at once justified by God, who raises him to a new spiritual life. But he who does not admit his sin-

---

[129] Hans Thimme, *Christi Bedeutung fuer Luthers Glauben* (Guetersloh, 1933), gives a fine account of Luther's thoughts on the exemplar-idea in the lectures on Romans, 1515—16. The same applies naturally to the lectures on the Psalms.

Vogelsang, *op. cit.*, pp. 98 ff., notes that Christ as a pattern, exemplar, is something different from Christ as an example in a moralistic sense. We cannot agree, however, with Vogelsang's view that Luther's idea of Christ as a pattern of the ways of God with men was something new and must be understood in the light of his evangelical conception of justification. This idea was not new, but simply one of the central thoughts of Augustine, LeFevre, and the Mystics. In fact, it was only an application of tropological interpretation of Scripture.

[131] *Ibid.*, p. 301, 30. Ps. 53/54:3. — In his commentary on the Psalms, Augustine explains briefly that humility means that one has no desire to glory in himself (*nolle in se laudari*, Migne, *op. cit.*, Vol. 36, pp. 309 f.). The thought is the same as that of Luther. Augustine also speaks of self-accusation. Luther follows him in his glossa of Ps. 50/51:8. — Hamel, *op. cit.*, I, 47.

Luther's First Lectures on the Psalms 63

fulness makes God a liar and robs Him of His honor. Such a one cannot be justified by God. The Biblical foundation of this thought is Ps. 51:6. Luther says:

"For it is impossible that he who confesses his sin would not be righteous, since he tells the truth. . . . But it is evident that sins will not be remitted to those who do not accuse themselves; neither are they raised again nor justified." [132]

Sometimes Luther says that humility makes man suitable and worthy to be justified and to receive grace:

"The more profoundly one condemns and magnifies his sins, the more fit *(aptus)* he is for the mercy and grace of God.[133]

"For while you are not in hell *(inferno)* or in death, you may assuredly fear the wrath of God and not yet hope in His mercy. For you are not yet worthy and fit *(dignus et aptus)* that He might have mercy upon you" [134] . . . "and so humbled they become fit for the mercy of God." [135]

The fundamental conception of Luther is that humility is divinely wrought conviction of sin and awareness of one's utter dependence on the grace of God. Alongside this insight there are, nonetheless, some remnants of the Catholic idea of meritorious disposition on the part of man. Luther emphasizes, however, that a truly humble person does not regard himself humble, but is in anguish on account of his sinfulness.[136]

In the lectures on the Psalms justification means *renewal* or *making righteous*. Following Augustine, Luther states:

"God saves the ungodly, as Augustine says, when He makes them pious and right in heart and when He keeps those who are already saved. Or He . . . brings to the goal of salvation . . . those

---

[136] Hirsch, *op. cit.*, p. 159, holds that the idea that when man "justifies God by confessing his sins, God justifies him" contains the reformation insight into justification. Loofs, "Der articulus stantis et cadentis ecclesiae," *op. cit.*, pp. 360, 405, makes the same assertion. Hamel, *op. cit.*, II, 136, is right in denying this. The judgment of Iwand, *op. cit.*, pp. 68, 76, agrees with him. This idea fits well the Augustinian conception of justification and not only the evangelical one.

who say: I hope to have my help from Thee, who art the Savior of the pious and a just God." [137]

In this statement justification is clearly spoken of as an *"analytic proposition."* First God makes man righteous, and then declares him such.

Luther sees no conflict between such a process of justification and the retributive justice of God. Following soon after the above statement, we have these thoughts:

"Justice . . . recompenses to each his due . . . equity distinguishes between merits, justice rewards. God judges the earth with equity (because He is the same to all, willing that all should be saved). He judges with righteousness, because He gives each one his deserved reward.[138]

The context of this statement is the exposition of a passage which speaks of God as the God who punishes the wicked and saves the pious. The Psalmist praises God for having rescued him from the hands of the wicked.[139]

The phrase "the righteousness of God," which caused Luther great difficulties, appears in Pss. 30/31:2 and 70/71:2. These passages Luther explains in the spirit of Augustine. In his exposition of Ps. 30/31:2 he passes over the words "deliver me in righteousness" with brief note, "not in mine, which is nothing."

---

[139] Hirsch, *op. cit.*, pp. 105 ff., and Vogelsang, *op. cit.*, pp. 30 f., state that Luther here presents the scholastic conception of righteousness and that these passages, therefore, belong to the time when he did not identify the righteousness and grace of God. This interpretation is hardly correct, for (1) the scholastic view of the righteousness of God did identify it and the grace of God (when it has this meaning in the text), as we have seen, and (2) Luther deals here with a passage in which the Psalmist speaks of the retributive justice of God. No other interpretation of these words is possible without doing violence to the text. One receives the impression from Hirsch and Vogelsang that Luther should have interpreted the phrase "the righteousness of God" to mean the grace of God regardless of whether it has that meaning in the text or not. — Scripture, as is well known, uses this term in both of these meanings, and it must be recognized by all sound exegesis, whether Catholic or Evangelical.

While interpreting Ps. 70/71:2, Luther has occasion to speak more at length of the "righteousness of God."

"The righteousness of God is wholly this, namely, that one humbles himself profoundly. . . . Here he speaks properly of Christ, who is the power and righteousness of God through the greatest and profoundest humility." [140]

"The tropological judgment of God . . . is that by which God condemns us and causes us to condemn what we are of ourselves, the old man as a whole, with all his works (even our righteousness, Isaiah 64). And so humility is actually humiliation. . . . For this is called the judgment of God, as the righteousness, power, and wisdom of God are those by which we are wise, strong, righteous, and humble, or judged." [141]

"All Scripture should be understood tropologically. The truth, wisdom, salvation, righteousness, are those by which He makes us strong, saved, righteous, wise, etc. So the works of God and the ways of God are all in the literal sense Christ. In the moral sense, all this is faith in Him. . . . Actually the Old Law only prophesied the first advent of Christ, in which He reigns in a benign and salutary judgment, because it is the advent of grace and lovingkindness. Therefore the Apostle says in Romans 3, 'The righteousness of God . . . through Jesus Christ.'" [142]

"No one can . . . 'be delivered by the righteousness of God' unless he hopes in the God who justifies the ungodly. . . . He does not say that he desires to be freed by something else besides righteousness. For we are delivered from unrighteousness by righteousness, just as we are delivered from sickness by health, and from ignorance by knowledge. Then he continues: 'and rescue me,' that is, from this body or with regard to this body. For even after the soul has been freed through righteousness, we are still in the dangers and exile of this life by reason of the body." [143]

---

[143] WA. 3, 453; cf. p. 443, 10. — The passages quoted nearly exhaust the ones in which Vogelsang, *op. cit.*, pp. 50 ff., finds the first clear expression of Luther's new conception of the righteousness of God and justification.

The thoughts of Luther as expressed in these statements are in perfect harmony with Augustine's commentary on the Psalms.[144] It is interesting to compare with the above the explanation of Ps. 70/71:2 as found in the commentary of Augustine, who says:

"Deliver me in Thy righteousness." Not in mine, but in Thine. . . . For what is mine? Iniquity precedes. And when I am righteous, it is by Thy righteousness, for I am righteous by the righteousness which Thou hast given. And so it is mine in order that it may be Thine, that is, given by Thee. For I believe in Him who justifies the ungodly, in order that my faith may be reckoned for righteousness."[145]

Luther was not required to discover the interpretation of the "righteousness of God," *iustitia Dei,* as the grace of God by which He makes man righteous, in contrast to His "active," retributive justice. It was clearly set forth in the commentary of Augustine, which he used in his exposition. Furthermore, it was the common property of the Church as the prevailing interpretation of almost all of the exegetes before and during the time of Luther.

From his words that "we are delivered from unrighteousness by righteousness, just as we are relieved from sickness by health, and from ignorance by knowledge," it is evident that in these lectures Luther understands justification to be a gradual healing from the corruption of sin by the power of grace. This process of justification Luther illustrates by the parable of the good Samaritan, who tended the wounded man and cured him.

"The Samaritan keeps us continually in the house where he relieves the pain (viz., of the conscience) with the oil of grace and gradually heals the sickness through the care of the innkeeper."[146]

The believer has only started to become righteous. He is striving toward the goal of perfect righteousness. "We are always sinning,

---

[144] Both Hamel, *op. cit.,* I, 166 f., and Vogelsang, *op. cit.,* p. 46, admit that Luther follows Augustine in his interpretations.

we are always impure . . . wherefore we who are righteous are constantly on the move, always being justified. . . . The starting point is sin, from which we must constantly depart. The goal is righteousness, toward which we must move unceasingly." [147]

The fact of his continued sinfulness makes it impossible for the Christian to consider himself justified in this life. He must be constantly occupied with striving toward the goal of righteousness.

"Those who are proud do not long to desire the justification of the Lord. . . . To long and desire for justification is to will, to pant ardently for justification and to be unwilling to reckon oneself ever to have apprehended it." [148]

Luther's conception of justification in these statements is typically Augustinian. It means a gradual "becoming righteous" by the work of divine grace; not that a sinner is "imputed or accounted righteous" for the sake of Christ. To be sure, Luther speaks of imputation, but he does not see it in the same light in which he sees it in his mature period. To reckon as righteous *(reputare iustum)* means the same as to be righteous before God. At times this term is used to signify appreciation or judgment of works. [149] It continues to be an "analytical" rather than a "synthetic" proposition.

True, Luther speaks of non-imputation of sins and of imputation of righteousness for the sake of Christ *(propter Christum)*, or because of faith in Christ. The emphasis, however, is on what Christ works *in* man. It is this that he has in mind when he occasionally uses the prepositional phrase "because of" or "for the sake of" *(propter)*:

". . . because of faith in Christ, who dwells in him." ". . . for the sake of Christ in us through faith." ". . . because of faith in Christ." [150]

All of these phrases refer to Christ and His work of renewal in and through faith. [151]

Luther is already aware of the fact that forgiveness is to be obtained as an undeserved gift. "Nobody can merit forgiveness of sin, but God remits sins by His gracious non-imputation." [152] Believers "have sins, but for the sake of Christ they shall not be imputed to them." [153]

Justification does not actually take place for the sake of Christ or on the basis of His atoning sacrifice. The suffering, death, and resurrection of Christ are primarily a "pattern" of how God deals with men.

"As He was offered on the Cross, so must we also be offered in a similar manner on the cross. . . ." [154] The Cross and sufferings of Christ are those vile and abject things in the world, such as humility, ignominy. . . . In them we are offered to God, even as Christ was on the Cross. They are the crosses, sufferings, and altars on which we present our bodies as a living sacrifice." [155]

The important thing in the tropological interpretation of the sacrifice of Christ is that it is both the pattern and the cause for man's sacrificing and surrendering himself to God. From another point of view it is also the key to the understanding of the work of God in man. Thereby is revealed how God saves man from the corruption of sin into the likeness of Christ.[156]

Naturally enough, Luther's conception of the Law corresponds with his understanding of justification. He writes:

"Spiritually understood, the Law and the Gospel are the same." [157]

"All that pertains only to the body and the senses and not to the spirit is letter. . . . But the new Law conveys spritual gifts and grace, by which the carnal and literal things are made void." [158]

Luther considers the Law from the ethical point of view. The Old Testament Law commands but does not give power for its ful-

---

[156] Bohlin, *op. cit.*, p. 349, is right in saying that, although Christ has an important place in justification in these lectures, His significance is no matter of principle. Although Luther emphasizes the necessity of faith in Christ, he does not think of justification as taking place *for the sake of Christ*. Still less does he mean by it the imputation of the atoning work of Christ to the sinner as righteousness. He understands justification in a more "theocentric" sense (*teocentriskt bestaemd*).

fillment. The New Testament, on the other hand, creates a new will and new power, making it possible for man willingly to observe the Law of God. The Old Testament Law is external, pertaining to the body and outward things. But the New Testament Law, that is, the Gospel, changes the heart and so makes the Law "spiritual."

Luther does not as yet know the distinction between the Law and the Gospel, which is so essential for his Reformation conception of justification. Further evidence of this is the fact that he understands the relationship between the Law and the Gospel according to the Augustinian formula of "shadow-reality."

"All that the Law says and does is but mere words and signs. The works of the Gospel, however, are the works and the reality thus signified." [159]

"All the works of creation and of the old Law are signs that point to the works of God in Christ and in His saints. Therefore all those acts are fulfilled like signs in Christ, for all of them are transitory, signifying those things which are eternal and permanent." [160]

Here is very apparent an admixture of Neo-Platonic thoughts and Biblical ideas. The relationship between the Law and the Gospel is seen as a contrast between shadow and reality, between the transitory and the permanent, the non-existing and the truly existing.

Further, Luther sees the Gospel as "flowing" out of the Law:

"The Gospel was hidden in the Law and thus invisible, as water in a rock, until Christ rent it and broke it open.[161]

"The new Law was hidden, concealed in the old Law, but it was expected to be brought forth and revealed by the coming Christ." [162]

These words remind one very definitely of the statement of Luther in his table talk that prior to his tower experience he made no distinction between Moses and Christ "except in regard to time and perfection."

The significant defect in this interpretation is that no distinction is made between the Ceremonial-judicial and the Moral Law. In his Reformation teaching Luther applies the "shadow-reality" formula only to the relationship between the Ceremonial-judicial Law and the New Covenant. The relationship between the Old Testament Moral Law and the fulfillment in Christ he expresses in a different manner.

We must conclude that — in spite of some minor differences between Augustine and Luther [163] — Luther's conception of justification and the relationship between the Law and the Gospel is essentially Augustinian. His final discovery of the nature and meaning of justification and its relationship to sanctification was still in the future. Had his doctrine remained as it was brought forth in the lectures on the Psalms, the Roman Church might have excommunicated him on the basis of certain "errors," but the Council of Trent would never have found it necessary to pronounce its anathema against a "Lutheran" doctrine of justification.[164]

[164] Roman Catholic Luther research has reached this same conclusion. So already Denifle, *op. cit.* I, 74. H. Grisar, *Luther* I (translated by E. M. Lamond; St. Louis and London, 1913), pp. 76 f., says that the passages in which Luther speaks of the non-imputation of sins and of the imputation of righteousness — in which many Protestant scholars have discovered a typically "Lutheran" teaching — contain no definite denial of the Catholic doctrine.

"Still, taken in their context, none of these passages furnish any decisive proof of a deviation from the Church's faith. They forbode, indeed, Luther's later errors, but contain as yet no explicit denial of the Catholic doctrine. In this we must subscribe to Denifle's view, and admit that no teaching actually heretical is found in the Commentary on the Psalms."

Grisar says that "the most suspicious passage in the Commentary on the Psalms is WA. 4, 227, which points to the continuance of his doubts regarding predestination; he says that Christ had drunk of the chalice of suffering for the elect, but not for all." Thus "the most suspicious passage" does not pertain to justification, but to predestination.

Grisar's general appraisal and criticism of Luther's lectures on the Psalms is essentially correct. He says that Luther's basic conception in them is Au-

Luther's First Lectures on the Psalms

The teaching of Luther in his first lectures on the Psalms is immature at three significant points:

1. He understands justification as a change of heart in man, that is, as a gradual renewal. Therefore he teaches that man can never reach the point where he can say that he is already righteous. It will remain a matter of becoming righteous.

2. He does not as yet possess a clear understanding of imputation. True, he speaks of it, but his conception of it does not correspond with his mature view.

3. The proper distinction between the Law and the Gospel is unknown to Luther. He is still in the phase of his development in which he does not make a distinction between Moses and Christ except as to time and perfection, as he says in one of his table talks.

These are the very truths of the Christian doctrine which Luther, according to his own statement, discovered in his tower experience.[165]

The only possible conclusion in the light of these facts is that during the period 1513—15 the tower experience of Luther had not yet occurred, but lay in the future.

Most Luther scholars have been and still are convinced that the tower experience of Luther transpired before the commencement of his lectures on the Psalms or at least in the course of them. They have, however, met with serious difficulties in their efforts to substantiate such a view.

Vogelsang tries to establish as a fact that Luther discovered his new interpretation of the Scriptural term "the righteousness of God" in the course of his lectures on the Psalms during 1513—15. He finds the first clear expression of this new insight in the ex-

---

gustinian, although there are influences from the Occamistic theology and Mysticism and some original ideas. "There is something unfinished about the work, because the author himself was still feeling his way towards that great alteration which he had at heart."

position of Psalm 71. Nevertheless, Vogelsang is forced to make the admission that in these lectures justification "is still conceived of as a process of becoming righteous in reality, that is, in the Augustinian sense, and not purely as an imputation of righteousness by God." Consequently he is confronted with the question "whether . . . the doctrine of justification in the lectures on the Psalms is of a pre-Reformation type at a decisive point." [166] This difficulty he attempts to escape by declaring that such a problem has resulted from a misunderstanding of Luther's later doctrine of justification. For "justification and making righteous belong closely together," he says, quoting Holl. "They are related to one another as the means and the goal. . . . God, who is eternal and almighty, sees that which comes into reality in the end as already present in the beginning, that is, when He pronounces the judgement . . . , for what God begins, He also brings to completion." Vogelsang then continues in his own words: "Holl's interpretation of the doctrine of imputation in the lectures on Romans holds true in all essential points also of the lectures on the Psalms. The essential thing in the matter is the inseparable unity of God's pronouncing righteous *(reputare iustum)* and making righteous *(efficere iustum)*."

Thus Vogelsang bases his assertion — that Luther discovered the evangelical conception of justification in the course of his lectures on the Psalms during 1513—14 — on the assumption that Holl's interpretation of Luther's Reformation doctrine of justification is correct. Unless one accepts this interpretation of Holl and his school, it is impossible to find Luther's mature doctrine of justification in these lectures. In that case one must go one step further and conclude that Luther's discovery of his final insight into justification had not yet taken place when he concluded his first course on the Psalms.

H. Wendorf is justified in making the statement that the theological prejudice of scholars has determined in a definite way the results of their investigation into the development of Luther. He

Luther's First Lectures on the Psalms 73

himself accepts the view that Luther's tower experience occurred before his first lecture course. However, he admits that these lectures contain not a trace of the "passive righteousness of God," as Luther understood it in his maturity. Therefore, Wendorf says, if this concept was the essential content of his discovery in the tower, a large portion of recent Luther research in this field must be rejected. Consequently the efforts of such men as Boehmer, Hirsch, Vogelsang, Scheel, and others to determine the time of Luther's discovery have been a complete failure. There is but one alternative, Wendorf concludes: either the aged Luther was wrong in stating that his discovery took place in 1518, or a considerable part of recent Luther research has missed the mark in its contention that it occurred as early as 1512—14.[167]

Wendorf touches the very heart of the matter in setting such an alternative. Contrary to what one might expect, however, he does not draw the conclusion that much of modern Luther research has gone astray in maintaining that the Reformer's final conception of justification is to be found in these lectures of 1513—15.[168]

As we proceed with our study, we hope to show just when the new insight does appear for the first time in Luther's writings.

---

[168] Hamel, *op. cit.*, I, 161, admits that Luther's conception of justification in these lectures is Augustinian. Nevertheless he assumes that the discovery of the Reformation doctrine of justification occurred before or during these lectures. He does not regard the results of Hirsch and Vogelsang as final, but believes that the problem of the date of the discovery may be solved through a careful study of the manuscript. — We venture to say that even a microscopic scrutiny of the manuscript will not reveal the first appearance of the new insight, because the only conception of justification to be found in these lectures is the Augustinian. — Bohlin, *op. cit.*, p. 354, concedes that Luther's teaching of justification in these lectures does not agree with the new insight he found through Rom. 1:16-17.

6

Luther's Lectures on Romans, 1515—1516

LUTHER began lecturing on Paul's Epistle to the Romans almost immediately after he had given his final lecture on the Psalms. In fact, he may not even have completed the first lectures before he undertook the new course.[169] It is only natural, therefore, that the two are akin in regard to doctrinal content.

The lectures on Romans reveal a greatly extended acquaintance with the writings of Augustine. Already the scholion to Rom. 2:12 contains a quotation from Augustine's treatise *On the Spirit and the Letter*. Later on in his lectures, Luther has occasion to quote several times from the same treatise.[170] He believes to have found in the writings of Augustine a congenial understanding of Paul's teaching of justification.

At the time when Luther was lecturing on Romans, the Greek New Testament was published (in February, 1515) with "Annotations" by the editor, Erasmus of Rotterdam. Luther used it for the first time in his exposition of the ninth chapter of Romans (WA. 56, 89 f.). He criticized the "annotations" of Erasmus, because they explain that Paul, in speaking of the freedom of the Christian from the Law, has in mind only the Ceremonial Law. Already then Luther knew that man cannot be justified without

---

[169] According to Boehmer, *Luthers erste Vorlesung*, pp. 8 f., Luther lectured on the Psalms from about August 16, 1513, to October 20, 1515, and on Romans from November 3, 1515, to September 9, 1916. Joh. Ficker (Preface to his edition of Luther lectures on Romans, p. XVI) says that Luther began his lectures on Romans already around Easter, 1515.

faith, simply by fulfilling the Moral Law.[171] However, as yet it had not entered into his thoughts that also the works which a Christian accomplishes in faith have no place in justification before God.

Already in the early phase of his monastic life, Luther was acquainted with a considerable amount of Mystical literature, such as Areopagite, Hugo and Richard of St. Victor, Bernhard of Clairvaux, Bonaventura, Gerson, and Bridget of Sweden. In the course of his lectures on Romans, Luther came in contact with the "German Mysticism" represented by Johann Tauler and the "Frankfort Anonymous," author of *German Theology (Eyn Deutsch theologia)*, which he found and published in 1516, supplying it with a preface of his own.[172]

German Mysticism found a strongly sympathetic response in the soul of Luther, because of the fact that it condemned all thoughts of human merit and rewards based on such merit. He was in full agreement with its view that sin is primarily a fault and perversity of the will of man. It is selfishness, love of sin, and repugnance toward the will of God. The teaching of man's complete passivity and utter helplessness in the matter of salvation also appealed to Luther. He found much in the writings of these Mystics that substantiated his emphasis upon humility, self-accusation, and self-condemnation. Tauler and the *German Theology* taught with Luther that before man can receive the grace of God and be born again, he must be convicted of his sins and experience anguish and pangs of conscience, fear and even despair. Man can never taste heaven unless he first tastes hell. Here he travels the way of Christ and becomes conformed to Him *(conformitas Christi)*. Such afflictions are to be considered, therefore, as signs of divine election, for that is the way in which God prepares His elect for salvation. Man needs to surrender to the will of God in unreserved humility. This *Gelassenheit*, that is, complete passivity and willing submission to the will of God in all things, is the right attitude of man before God. The sufferings and death of Christ are the noblest examples of true *Gelassenheit*. As such they are the pattern of God's dealings with man. In their doctrine of justification these Mystics were disciples of Augustine, teaching that God justifies man by making him righteous. The soul experiences heavenly bliss and sabbath rest already in this life when man is emptied of that which is original with him and the world and when Christ is born in his heart.[173]

Both medieval Scholasticism and Mysticism taught that there remains in man an uncorrupted divine kernel. However, they explained it somewhat differently. According to Scholasticism the human conscience is liable to temptations and afflictions; but in the depths of the soul is a *synteresis* which continues untouched by the depravity caused by the fall into sin. The orientation of this divine kernel is permanently toward God and away from sin. Medieval Mystics spoke of the "basis of the soul" *(Seelengrund)* where God abides at all times. The scholastic *synteresis* had its origin in the creative work of God, while *Seelengrund* was the product of the infused grace. However, at this point there is some overlapping between the scholastic and the mystic doctrines.[174]

The primary reason why Luther admired the works of the Mystics was that his own conception of salvation was still very closely related to theirs. He found that their works confirmed him in his

---

[174] The distinction between conscience (Greek, *syneidesis*) and synteresis originated in an error of a copyist in Jerome's exposition of Ez. 1:4-10. A copyist had written *synteresis* instead of *syneidesis*. See Nitsch, "Eine bestaetigte Konjectur. Historischer Beitrag zur Lehre vom Gewissen," *Zeitschrift fuer Kirchengeschichte*, 1897—98, p. 29; *Die Lehre der Scholastiker von der Synteresis* (1891), p. 2; according to L. Pinomaa, *Luther-tutkielmia* (Helsinki, 1938), pp. 94 ff. — *Synteresis*, as an uncorrupted kernel in man, fitted well into the Semi-Pelagian scholastic theology. — As yet Luther saw no difference between the Mystics and Paul. This is evident from his letter to Spalatin in 1516 (Enders 1, 75): "If you take any pleasure at all in reading theology that is pure, solid, and most similar to ancient theology written in the German tongue, then read the sermons of Johann Tauler. . . . For neither in Latin nor in our language have I found a purer and more wholesome theology nor any that agrees better with the Gospel."

conviction that the way of humility, self-denial, and the cross is the true way that leads to God.

In his exposition of Romans, Luther continued to use the formula which required him to find a fourfold meaning in Scripture. As a result his interpretations resemble very closely those found in his earlier lectures. The text with which he was now concerned, however, was much more specifically Christian than the Old Testament Psalms, so that of necessity he had to pay more attention to the central truths of the Christian faith, in particular to the doctrine of justification.

Early in his lectures, Luther still speaks of *synteresis* in the traditional manner.[175] Also the second time he mentions it, he still admits that man possesses some power for good,[176] but when the matter comes to his attention the third time,[177] he explicitly denies that *synteresis*, that "tiny movement" in man, can be righteousness. Human nature as such has no general ability to know and to will the good *(in genere universali nosse et velle bonum),* even though at times and to an extent that may be the case.[178]

In Luther's attitude toward the doctrine of *synteresis* we see the trend of these lectures as a whole. He continues to follow the path of traditional theology in many points, but simultaneously he approaches by degrees his final insight into the Christian Gospel.

The purpose of the Law, Luther teaches, is not to better man, but to reveal to him his sin, that he may yearn and pray for grace, "groan before God and, humbled, pray that God may restore his will."[179] Self-accusation and prayer for grace are the prerequisites or conditions of justification. The Law having convicted man of his sinfulness, he "sighs to God and humbly asks to be raised and his will to be cured. He, however, who does not realize his sinfulness will not ask."[180]

God is righteous in Himself. Consequently He does not justify the sinner unless the sinner first justifies Him by confessing that God is true and just when in His Word He judges the sinner. Thereby God "becomes righteous also in us."[181]

The only thing that can restore the sick will of man and enable it to fulfill the Law in a free and willing spirit is divine grace. Thereby the grace of God also creates in man an "inner righteousness." [182] "The will is healed in order that we may be free and joyful in doing the works of the Law, asking nothing but to please God and to do His will, acting neither of fear nor of selfishness." [183]

To support these thoughts, Luther gathers several quotations from Augustine's treatise *On the Spirit and the Letter*.[184] With Augustine, Luther says that the moment man, humbled by the Law, longs for and seeks righteousness, he is already "righteous to some extent" *(aliquo modo iustus)*.[185]

"For he who seeks it from heart and by work is beyond doubt righteous in the sight of God by the very fact that he endeavors to be justified and does not regard himself as already righteous." [186]

There can be no mistake about the Augustinian conception of justification in the following statement: "The righteousness which we have from God is the very inclination toward good and aversion toward evil, inwardly given by grace; but works are the fruits of righteousness." [187] This renewal into a righteous man never reaches perfection in this life. Righteous acts promote this advancement or growth in righteousness. "Works which are righteous and done in grace are always a preparation for the following step in the advancement in righteousness, as it is written: 'He that is righteous is justified further.' " [188]

The very heart of his conception of justification Luther reveals in the following statements:

"The . . . believing people, the spiritual people . . . beseech, ask, and beg to be justified constantly until death." [189]

"No one among the living loves righteousness without also to some extent loving iniquity. So we are partly righteous but not entirely. . . . For the proneness to evil is not perfectly removed in this life." [190]

"Man is always in a state of unfinished business; he is always about to become. . . . He is in sin as to his starting point and in righteousness as to his goal. Thus, being constantly penitent, we are always sinners; but by that very fact we are, nevertheless, righteous and being justified. We are partly sinners, partly righteous." [191]

"Man is justified more and more, no one is righteous" here on earth.[192] He may be compared to a sick man who is being restored to health under the care of a physician. In reality he is still sick, but he is on the road to recovery:

"For He has not as yet justified us, that is, perfected and finished the righteousness and the righteous ones, but He has begun it in order to bring it to perfection. . . . As revealed in the case of the man who was nearly dead when given to the care of the innkeeper. He was not yet healed of the wounds that had been inflicted, but he was being provided the proper cure" *(Non enim justificavit nos, i. e., perfecit et absolvit iustos ac iustitiam, sed incepit ut perficiat. . . .).* [193]

God does not condemn the Christian because of the sins that remain while He is carrying on justification or the healing of human nature:

"Our Samaritan, Christ, takes a sick man, who is practically dead, into the inn to heal him. He has already begun to make him well, promising perfect health in eternal life and not imputing sin, that is, concupiscence, for death. Meanwhile He prohibits, in the hope of health that is promised, such doing and omitting of things as hinder that cure and increase sin, that is, the evil lust." [194]

The gracious imputation of God supplements or covers that which is lacking in the righteousness of man while the process of becoming righteous is going on. The believer is righteous only in so far as the Physician pronounces him cured, although actually the restoration is not yet accomplished but only begun.

"He is simultaneously sick and well. Sick in reality but well in the light of the sure promise of the Physician in whom he trusts and who regards him as well, because He is sure that He will cure him for the reason that He has already begun to do so and has not imputed the sickness to him for death." [195]

The phrase "simultaneously sick and well" is identical with the phrase "simultaneously sinful and righteous." The meaning, however, is this, that the Christian is partly righteous, or renewed, and partly unrighteous, or depraved.

"Is he . . . perfectly righteous? No, but he is at once a sinner and righteous: a sinner in reality but righteous on the basis of the sure imputation and promise of God that He will deliver him from sin and finally cure him perfectly." [196]

The non-imputation of the sins that remain, Luther points out, takes place on account of *(propter)* the commenced cure. Elsewhere he says that it is based on the confession of sins and self-accusation.

"No saint considers himself, or professes to be, righteous, but constantly longs and waits for justification. On this account they are imputed righteous by God, who looks upon those who are humble. Thus Christ is the King of the Jews, that is, of those who confess that they remain continually in sin. Nevertheless, they possess in their hearts a desire for justification, and they abhor their sins. Therefore God is wonderful in His saints, for He reckons righteous those who acknowledge that they are sinners and experience sorrow on that account; but he condemns those who regard themselves as righteous." [197] Thus in themselves and in reality they are unrighteous; nevertheless, they are righteous, because God reckons them such for the sake of this confession of sin. Actually they are sinners, but through the imputation of God they are righteous; unknowingly righteous and knowingly unrighteous; sinners in reality, but righteous in hope. . . . Behold, every saint is a sinner and prays on account of his sins. . . . The grace of God is, therefore, most wonderful and sweet, for He reckons us at the same time sinful and sinless." [198]

"Sin exists in reality, but God remits it through His gracious non-imputation to all who acknowledge it, confess and hate it, desiring to be freed from it. Thus we are sinners in ourselves; and yet we are righteous through faith, since God reckons us such on account of our faith in Him who promises that He will deliver us from sin." [199]

At times Luther speaks of the non-imputation of sins as taking place for Christ's sake, because His righteousness "covers" the penitent and believing sinner and is imputed to him.

"The saints are sinners at the same time that they are righteous. They are righteous because they believe in Christ, whose righteousness covers them and is imputed to them *(iusti quia credunt in Christum, cuius iustitia eos tegit et eis imputatur).* They are sinners, because they do not fulfill the Law and are not free from evil lust. They are like sick men under the cure of a physician: in reality they are sick, and yet they are on the road to recovery and well in hope. . . . They are being cured, that is, they are about to become well." [200]

"Their radical sin is not taken into account. . . . It is covered . . . by Christ, who dwells in us." [201]

"They know that they have sin, but it is covered for the sake of Christ, and it is not imputed, in order that all this good may be outside of them in Christ, who, however, is in them through faith." [202]

Here Luther speaks of the non-imputation of sins for the sake of Christ. However, justification does not mean the imputation of the fulfillment of the Law accomplished by Christ or of His righteousness. The manner of expression here is typically Augustinian. Christ covers the remaining sins. The real healing or renewal which has begun is, at least in part, the basis of the non-imputation. God reckons man healthy and well, because He has started to make him such and has given the sure promise that He will bring it to perfection.

"To be sure, he is still a sinner, but he is not ungodly *(non impius).* For such a one is called ungodly who is not a servant of God, but is turned away from Him and is without fear and reverence for God. But he who is justified and whose sin is covered is already converted and pious, for he serves God and seeks Him in hope and fear. And because of this *(per hoc)* God imputes him pious and righteous.... For to such is imputed not impiety, but piety, because there is no guile within them, which of necessity is found in those who do not reckon themselves impious, even though their sins and wickedness are not covered and remitted by God." [203]

Since the believers are already servants of God and pious, that is, righteous in principle in their hearts and lives, God credits them with righteousness for the reason of this commenced renewal and does not impute their sins for guilt.

These quotations are taken almost exclusively from the exposition of such passages in Romans in which Paul definitely and clearly speaks of the imputed righteousness and not of being made righteous.[204] Yet Luther – following Augustine – interprets them to mean the gradual process of becoming righteous. The non-imputation of the sins that remain is simply a supplement to this sanative justification. Fundamentally justification is an "analytic" proposition: God reckons righteous those whom He has made righteous.[205]

Luther's basic conception of justification is as yet essentially Augustinian or about the same as that which is expressed in his lectures on the Psalms. Here and there is found evidence of a

---

[205] Taito A. Kantonen, *Resurgence of the Gospel* (Philadelphia, Pa., 1948), pp. 50 f., is right in rejecting Karl Holl's interpretation of Luther's doctrine of justification, but he makes the mistake (made by most Luther scholars) that he believes to find this mature doctrine in the lectures on Romans. Kantonen says that in such passages in which Luther uses the illustration of a patient who is in the care of a physician, he does not describe justification, but the daily sanctification of the believer already living in grace. This would apply to Luther's mature teaching, but in his lectures on Romans he certainly speaks of justification in such passages. Kantonen, referring to our present study, gives the correct view in the footnote, but not in the text. He had not read the study, but only heard of its contents.

deepening of insight, but even such deepening occurs within the framework of the Augustinian conception.

The distinction between "grace" and "gift" (*gratia, donum*) in these lectures on Romans is only distantly related to Luther's later teaching. He says:

"'The grace of God' by which He justifies us . . . and the 'gift' is that which Christ sends from the Father into those who believe in Him. This 'gift by grace' of that one Man is His personal grace and merit, for the sake of which it pleases God to grant that gift to us. The word 'by the grace of one Man' is to be understood to mean the personal grace of Christ. . . . The grace and gift of God are one, namely, the very righteousness freely bestowed through Christ." [206]

Here "grace" is not identical with imputation of righteousness for the sake of Christ, as Luther understands the term in his mature period. It is simply the basis or condition (the "meritorious cause") of the bestowal of the gift which makes man righteous (*qua Deo placuit, ut donum illud daret nobis*).

There are to be found in Luther's lectures on Romans certain statements which appear to reflect his mature understanding of justification. At the beginning of these lectures, Luther makes the statement that the intention of Paul in this Epistle is to destroy all self-righteousness and to replace it with "everything that is outside of us in Christ . . . , for God will not save us through our own native righteousness and wisdom, but through that which is extraneous; not through that which comes and is born of us, but which comes into us from the outside; not through that which rises from our earth, but which descends from heaven. Therefore an altogether extraneous and alien righteousness (*externa et aliena iustitia*) should be taught." [207]

However, this "extraneous and alien righteousness" is not the imputed righteousness of the mature Luther. Luther uses these words simply to show that the transformation of the sinful man into a righteous one is altogether the work of Christ.

The closest Luther approaches to his mature insight into justification is in the following statements.

"The righteousness of the saints is not the fulfillment of the Law, but the communication of Christ's fulfillment alone, which He has accomplished." [208]

When the Christian is accused in his heart because of his sins, he should turn to Christ and say:

"But He has supplied satisfaction, He is righteous, He is my Defender, He has died for me, He has made His righteousness mine and my sin His. And if He takes my sins upon Himself, then I do not have them any longer, and I am free. But if He has made His righteousness mine, . . . I am already righteous through the same righteousness as He. My sin cannot swallow Him, but is itself swallowed up in the abyss of His infinite righteousness." [209]

The level which Luther reaches with these thoughts is considerably above Augustine. If the insight into justification which they reveal were typical of the entire commentary, we would be obliged to say that Luther teaches in it his Reformation doctrine of justification. Throughout the lectures, however, he labors with the Augustinian conception of justification as a process of being made righteous. Consequently — regardless of the apparent tension between the two — we must understand these statements in the context of the lectures as a whole. They then mean that even though Christ has taken man under His justifying care, the actual righteousness of man is insignificant. He remains a sinner. Therefore it is necessary for him to put his trust in the merits of Christ and His righteousness. On their account God will not impute to him his remaining sins, while he is being cured and justified.

Augustine also says that the righteousness of the believer consists more in the forgiveness of sins than in the perfection of virtues, because his actual righteousness is very insignificant in this life. Both he and Luther use nearly identical phrases:

"The Christian's righteousness depends more on the imputation of God *(magis pendet ab imputatione Dei)* than on the fact of actual righteousness *(quam ab esse rei).* For mere quality does not make man righteous — rather, he is wholly sinful and unrighteous. But he is righteous whom God graciously reckons righteous, because he confesses his unrighteousness and prays for the righteousness of God. Such a one God graciously regards righteous in His sight. Therefore all of us are born and die in iniquity, that is, in unrighteousness. We are righteous only through the pure imputation of the merciful God by faith in Him." [210]

Typically Augustinian is the expression "depends more" and the statement that the "quality" or the renewal of the heart and life does not suffice because it is imperfect. When Luther goes on to say that the believers are righteous "through the pure imputation of the merciful God," we cannot understand his words rightly apart from the words "depends more," which serve as definite qualifiers. The gracious imputation of God as a supplement takes care of by far the greater portion of required righteousness.

Luther as yet considers and understands justification primarily from the ethical point of view:

"No one is . . . accounted righteous except he who fulfills the Law in deed. But no one fulfills it save he who believes in Christ. And so the Apostle concludes that apart from Christ no one is righteous, no one fulfills the Law." [211]

Here justification implies and means the creation of a new heart, which makes man capable of fulfilling the Law of God from a free and willing spirit. Such a heart is found only in a believer.

The same ethical point of view determines Luther's conception of the distinction between the flesh and the spirit in believers:

"The individual is both spirit and flesh. Consequently, whatever he does with the flesh is rightly said to be done by him as a whole. But when he resists it, however, it is proper to say that he does not do it as a whole; it is done by a part of him. . . . But since the carnal man as a whole consents to the law of the members, he acts as a whole self when he sins." [212]

True, Luther speaks of spirit and flesh in this ethical sense also in his mature period, but a further aspect has been added. Man is "flesh" in so far as he seeks righteousness in himself and through his own efforts; he is "spirit" in so far as he appropriates the righteousness of Christ, promised and imputed to him through the Gospel. In his lectures on Romans, Luther knows only the ethical point of view of sanctification.[213]

A further difference is evident in Luther's attitude toward the matter of assurance of salvation. In 1515–16, at the time of his lectures on Romans, he believes that a man can know with certainty only the fact of his sinfulness, and can only hope and postulate *(postulare et sperare)* God's imputation. Obviously the reason for this is that in 1515–16 Luther does not know the art of distinguishing aright between the Law and the Gospel. He does not understand that the fulfillment of the Law, which is accomplished in faith, is not an element in justification. He still teaches that justification means the fulfillment of the Law in man through grace.[214] As a consequence of this deficient distinction between the Law and the Gospel, Luther's certainty of salvation rests, at least to some extent, upon his progress in justification (sanctification). In practical piety his own humility, endeavors, prayers, and conduct enter in as partial condition for his acceptability before God. Therefore he is never able to feel quite safe and secure in the grace of God, inasmuch as he is unable to put his full reliance upon the "alien" righteousness of Christ.

In his lectures on Romans, Luther's conception of justification is still of the pre-Reformation type. The dominating aspect is the ethical one, not the religious.[215]

---

[215] Ruben Josefson, *Oedmjukhet och tro. En studie i den unge Luthers teologi* (Uppsala, 1939), holds the view that Luther's conception of justification in his lectures on Romans is mature in all essential points; he admits, however, that Luther speaks in these lectures of justification as a process of becoming righteous (p. 145). Yet he avers that in the doctrine of justification Luther is consistently evangelical. He holds that even in his mature period

Luther does not distinguish between justification and renewal in the manner of Melanchthon and the Lutheran Orthodoxy, but understands both as one indivisible work of God (p. 107). — It seems that Josefson comes to his "results" in part at least because he accepts the Hollian interpretation of the mature teaching of Luther. Josefson is a representative of the Lundensian interpretation of Luther. The school of Lund unites justification and sanctification so that they come to mean the same thing. — Professor Hjalmar Lindroth has his doubts about Josefson's "results" in his review of the latter's book, *Svensk Teologisk Kvartalskrift*, 1941, p. 166.

7

Luther's Conception of Justification in 1517—1518

SUBSEQUENT to the course of Romans, Luther lectured on Galatians (from October 27, 1516 to March 13, 1517) and also on Hebrews (from March 16, 1517, to March 27, 1518). His lectures on Galatians present nothing new in regard to justification, perhaps for the simple reason that in his previous lectures this doctrine had received special consideration. Also in his lectures on Hebrews Luther sets forth the same views as were expressed in the previous courses. The following statement is expressive of his understanding of justification: "Christians are righteous, holy, and free from sin, not because they are such but because they have started to and will become such by way of constant growth." [216]

About the time when he began his course of lectures on Hebrews, Luther published his first book, the explanation of the Seven Penitential Psalms. Its popularity demanded several editions within a few years. This book is worthy of special interest and attention for two reasons. It was published in the same year that witnessed the posting of the Ninety-Five Theses, just a few months earlier, and it became the means of broadcasting Luther's religious thoughts among the German people in the days of the dawn of the Reformation. When it first left the publishers, it carried with it the strong recommendation of Staupitz.[217]

Even a superficial study of this book shows that its dominating spirit is the same humility and piety which is characteristic of Lu-

Luther's Conception of Justification

ther's first lecture courses. The theme of the book is: Grace belongs to the humble. Contrary to what might be expected, Luther has but little more to add in regard to the grace and merciful imputation of God to what he had already said in his first course on the Psalms even in his explanation of Psalm 32:

"No one is free from unrighteousness. All are altogether unrighteous in the sight of God. No one is without evil deeds which are . . . quite apparent to God. But blessed is he whose sins He covers, willing not to see, think about, or know them, but forgives them purely out of grace." [218]

All that Luther says here had already been said by Augustine.

Explaining Psalm 51, Luther speaks of the gradual process of cleansing in the same manner as in his early lectures.

"He prays . . . that he may be washed and cleansed more and more. For the first grace signifies that the washing and cleansing has been started. . . . Adam must leave and Christ come in. Adam must be destroyed, and Christ alone must rule and exist. Therefore the washing and cleansing has no end in time." [219]

In his discussion of righteousness, Luther emphasizes the truth that it is the gracious gift of God and does not depend upon human merit. However, he does not define the content and meaning of this justifying grace. Nonetheless it is evident that he has in mind the renewing grace, here as elsewhere at this time: "He whom Thou doest not justify will never become righteous through his works." [220]

The year 1517 belongs to that period of Luther's life when he still understood justification as a renewal and a gradual cleansing from sin and not as the imputation of the righteousness of Christ.

However, this period marks an important development in Luther's theological thought. During 1516–1517 he rejected the Augustinian-Catholic theory of fourfold sense of Scripture *(Quadriga)* and began to interpret the Scriptures according to their literal meaning. Thus was severed one of the significant bonds that tied him to the traditional past.[221]

Toward the end of April, 1518, the German Augustinians held a convention in Heidelberg. For the disputation at this convention Luther drew up a number of theses which it was his task to defend. They reveal his conception of justification at that time.

Luther's primary interest in the Heidelberg disputations was to destroy all form of human righteousness and reliance on works, so that men would understand that salvation is of grace alone. Therein he goes deeper than before:

"The man who thinks that he can attain grace by doing what is in his power to do adds sin to sin, becoming doubly guilty."

Speaking of justification, Luther says:

"Not he who works much is righteous, but he who, without works, believes much in Christ. For the righteousness of God is not acquired by actions that are often repeated, as Aristotle taught, but it is infused through faith. . . . For grace and faith are infused without our works, but the works follow that infusion. . . . It is proper to say that the work of Christ is that which produces the works, and ours is that which is effected *(opus Christi dicetur operans, et nostrum operatum).*

"The love of God does not invent, but it creates the object of its love. Human love is born out of the object of his love. . . ."[222]

". . . the love of God which lives in man loves sinners, the evil ones, the stupid, the weak, in order to make them righteous, good, wise, and strong, and so it is indeed a love which flows forth and bestows blessings. For sinners are beautiful because they are loved. They are not loved because they are beautiful. . . . The love of the cross . . . does not go where it finds good that it can enjoy, but where it can bring blessings to such as are evil and in need. For it is more blessed to give than to receive."[223]

It cannot be denied that these thoughts are in harmony with Luther's final doctrine of salvation. Luther continues, however, to understand justification as renewal. Grace effects in man the willing spirit that the Law requires. The works of a believer are the product of the grace of God.

The Luther of the Heidelberg disputations knows as yet only the "second" part of the work of God, the renewal by the "gift of grace," and forgiveness as its supplement. In the spring of 1518 Luther's conception of justification still is of the Augustinian type.[224]

---

[224] Walter von Loewenich, *Luthers theologia crucis* (Muenchen, 1933), holds that in the Heidelberg disputations the theology of Luther is not of the pre-Reformation type. Y. J. E. Alanen, *op. cit.*, p. 26, is right in saying that this is true only "in some points." Reinhold Seeberg, *Lehrbuch der Dogmengeschichte* IV, 1 (4th edition, Leipzig, 1933), p. 82, asserts that in 1517 Luther's theology was perfectly clear in regard to its basic concepts and that in its kernel no further change took place. The same view is held by Edgar M. Carlson, *The Reinterpretation of Luther* (Philadelphia, Pa., 1948), p. 16. Carlson declares that Luther had arrived at his characteristic interpretation of the Gospel, his conception of sin and grace, and his doctrine of justification by faith alone, already prior to 1518. This is not true, as we have seen. In the case of Seeberg one need not be surprised at such a view, for his interpretation of Luther's Reformation doctrine of justification is closely akin to that of Karl Holl. Neither is it surprising in the case of Carlson, who in the main follows the Lundensian interpretation of Luther. — Gustaf Ljunggren, *Synd och skuld i Luthers teologi* (Uppsala, 1928), p. 46, remarks that at least until 1518 Luther's doctrine of justification belongs to the pre-Reformation type.

8

Luther's "Tower Experience" at the End of the Year 1518

PROBABLY toward the end of the year 1518 Luther published his "Sermon on the Threefold Righteousness" *(Sermo de triplici iustitia)*. In it he distinguishes three forms of sin and, correspondingly, three types of righteousness. The first of these is sin and righteousness according to the civil law. With its motives of fear of punishment and love of pleasure, it is no Christian righteousness, but a righteousness of Jews and Gentiles.

"The second sin is essential, inborn, original, alien, of which Psalm 51 says: 'Behold, I was shapen in iniquity, and in sin did my Mother conceive me.'

"The righteousness that corresponds to this is in a similar manner inborn, essential, original, alien — which is the righteousness of Christ *(natalis, essentialis, originalis, aliena, quae est iustitia Christi);* Romans 5: 'Through the act of righteousness of the one unto all men to justification of life, and through the obedience of the one shall the many be made righteous.'

"This is . . . our lot, capital, foundation, rock, and our whole substance wherein we glory forever, as the Apostle says that 'your life is hid with Christ in God,' and again: 'That we might become the righteousness of God in Him,' and 1 Corinthians 1: Who was made unto us from God both righteousness and sanctification and redemption.

"It becomes our own through faith, Romans 1: 'The righteous shall live by faith,' and Romans 10: 'With the heart man believeth unto righteousness.' It is that which the Gospel properly proclaims. It is not the righteousness of the Law, but the righteousness of Grace. . . .

"The Apostle says in Romans 5 that Adam is a figure of Him that was to come, namely, as Adam made all who were born of him guilty by the one sin, his own sin, which to them is an alien sin and gave them what he had, in the same manner Christ makes righteous and saves by His own righteousness all who are born of Him. To them it is alien and unmerited, in order that as we are condemned on account of an alien sin, so we may also be saved by an alien righteousness.

"I call it essential and eternal, because it endures forever. . . . Christ alone is eternal, therefore His righteousness also is eternal, and yet it is ours. This is the mercy of the Father; this is the grace of the New Testament, through which the Lord is sweet to them who taste Him. By it we must be saved, and by nothing else . . . Psalm 30 (31:2), 'Deliver me in Thy righteousness.' . . .

"The third is actual sin, which is the fruit of original sin. These are the sins proper, namely, all the works we do, even the works of righteousness which we accomplish prior to faith. . . .'

"The righteousness that corresponds to this is the actual righteousness, flowing out of faith and the essential righteousness. . . .

"Therefore, whether you sin or not, rely always upon Christ and that essential righteousness. . . . And so the works of such faith are most acceptable, even though in regard to you and in themselves they may be most unworthy." [225]

Before attempting to draw any conclusions, it is worth the effort to make a comparative summary and analysis of this lengthy quotation.

1. Original, essential, inborn, alien *sin* is received in the natural birth, without our own activity.	1. Original, essential, inborn *righteousness* is received in the new birth, without our own activitiy.

2. By his one sin Adam made all his descendants guilty and gave them what he had.

3. We are condemned through an alien sin.

4. The essential sin, inherited from Adam, never ceases, causing a continuous guilt.

5. Original sin is from without and therefore "alien," namely, Adam's sin imputed to us.

6. Original sin is our "lot," our evil "property" and eternal shame.

7. Actual sin is the fruit of original sin, which is its source.

8. Evil deeds do not cause the original sin, neither can good works destroy it. Original sin is prior to, and independent of, all works. It remains as long as unbelief remains, which makes all deeds sinful and blots out the value of good works, regardless of their outward value.

2. By His own righteousness Christ, the second Adam, makes righteous and saves all who are born of Him, without their own merits.

3. We are saved through an alien righteousness.

4. The essential righteousness, "inherited" from Christ is eternal, never ceasing, because Christ is eternal.

5. The "original" righteousness is from without and therefore "alien," namely, Christ's righteousness imputed to us.[226]

6. Christ's righteousness is our new "lot," our new blessed "capital" and eternal glory.

7. The actual righteousness of life and works is the fruit of the original or essential righteousness, which is its source.

8. Good deeds do not cause the original righteousness, neither can evil works in themselves destroy it. Original righteousness is prior to and independent of all works. It remains as long as faith in Christ remains, whose righteousness gives good works their value and blots out evil works.

The conception of justification which Luther sets forth in this sermon is in perfect harmony with his Reformation doctrine. The

---

[226] Luther does not actually use here the term "impute," but it expresses his meaning.

basic idea of righteousness before God, as expressed in it, is no longer compatible with the Augustinian view. Luther quite definitely teaches that man is justified through the eternal righteousness of Christ and not through a renewal or becoming righteous through the working of grace. The emphasis is laid on the work of Christ *for* sinners. In Him the believers have an adequate righteousness. The "actual" righteousness of life and works is the fruit of justifying faith.

Relying wholly upon the righteousness of Christ, Luther has now an altogether new tone in his whole life, a tone of trustful confidence and courage. It is no longer necessary for him to stop at wailing and mourning his sinfulness and praying for grace. He is able to believe confidently that grace is actually his and that he is already righteous before God through the merit of Christ.

Shortly after the above sermon, Luther published another on the same subject, "Sermon on the Twofold Righteousness *(Sermo de duplici iustitia)*.[227] This sermon contains an even clearer expression of his new insight:

"The righteousness of Christians" is twofold, even as the sin of men is twofold.

"The first is the alien one. . . . By it Christ is righteous and justifies us by faith, 1 Corinthians 1: 'Who was made unto us wisdom from God, and righteousness and sanctification and redemption.' . . . This righteousness is bestowed upon men in Baptism and every time they truly repent, so that man can confidently glory in Christ and say: All that Christ has accomplished by His

---

[227] We do not know why Luther published so soon another sermon on the same subject. Perhaps he was not quite satisfied with the first sermon, or perhaps his heart, overflowing with the new insight, urged him to speak of it again. — The exact time of the writing and publishing of this sermon is not known. Luther makes mention of it in his letter to Johann Lang, April 13, 1519, saying that an unauthorized edition in poor shape had been published. He himself produced a better edition. Apparently, therefore, Luther must have delivered the sermon not later than the first quarter of 1519 (WA. 2, 143).

work and Word, all the blessings of His suffering and death are mine, as if I had done it all, lived, acted, spoken, suffered, and died. A bridegroom has all that the bride has, and the bride all that belongs to the bridegroom. . . .

"Thus through faith in Christ the righteousness of Christ becomes our righteousness, and so all that He has, even He Himself, becomes ours. Therefore the Apostle calls it the righteousness of God, Romans 1: 'The righteousness of God is revealed in the Gospel, as it is written: The righteous shall live by faith.' This is an infinite righteousness, and it swallows up all sins in a moment *(omnia peccata in momento absorbens),* because it is impossible that sin should inhere in Christ. On the contrary, he who believes in Christ cleaves to Christ and is one with Christ, having the same righteousness as He has *(habens eandem iustitiam cum ipso).* Therefore it is impossible that sin should remain in him.

"It is thus that we are to understand Psalm 30: 'In Thee, O Lord, do I put my trust; I shall never be ashamed; deliver me in Thy righteousness.' He does not say 'in my,' but 'in Thy,' i. e., in the righteousness of Christ, my God. In other passages of the Psalter it is called the work of the Lord, the confession, the power of God, the mercy, the truth, the righteousness. All these are names for faith in Christ, yea, for the righteousness that is in Christ. Therefore the Apostle dares to say in Ephesians 3: 'That Christ may dwell in your hearts through faith.'

"Thus this alien righteousness, which is poured into us without our works, solely through grace . . . is set against the original sin, which is both alien and inborn, coming into us without our works, through birth alone. . . .

"The *second* righteousness is our own, and it is the proper one; not that we work it alone, but because we co-operate with that first and alien righteousness. This is that good conduct in good works, first in the mortification of the flesh and the crucifixion of evil lusts . . . secondly, also, in love toward our neighbor, and, thirdly, in humility and fear toward God. . . .

Luther's "Tower Experience"

"This righteousness is the work of the first righteousness, its fruit and effect. . . .

"This righteousness is set against the actual and real sin in us. . . .

"This is the Gospel and the example of Christ." [228]

The main thoughts of the earlier sermon are here repeated, but the distinction between the righteousness of faith and the righteousness of life is expressed more clearly. Several chief points are worth special attention:

1. Christ and His work from the manger to Calvary is the righteousness of believers. All sins are blotted out in a moment through this infinite righteousness. As an infinite righteousness it is the possession of man completely and immediately through faith.

2. The second righteousness is man's renewal through a gradual process of advancement and growth. It follows the first righteousness as its fruit and effect. This renewal into conformity with the image of Christ is not the result of a moment. The mortification of the flesh is gradual, and the fruits of the new spiritual man increase by the working of Christ in him.

3. In both sermons Luther makes reference to Ps. 31:2 and Rom. 1:17. He gives special attention in his latter sermon to Ps. 31:2. "It is thus," he says, "that we are to understand Psalm 30." These words seem to indicate that Luther had now discovered the right understanding of this passage. Using words almost identical with those in his *Preface* of 1545, he explains that this "righteousness of God" is the righteousness of Christ. It is bestowed upon the sinner through faith in Christ. — It is often called in the Psalms the work of the Lord, God's mercy, power, truth, righteousness. Luther states expressly that this righteousness, work, mercy, and truth of God is not the "second" righteousness or the gradual renewal of man, in heart and life, into the image of Christ. It is the "first" or "alien" righteousness which is bestowed upon sinners completely at once. It means that the guilt of sin is blotted out through the forgiveness of sins. The

righteousness of Christ, apprehended by faith, immediately covers all sins.[229] Thereby man becomes Christ's own, and Christ his. He is a child of God and an heir of eternal life.

The second righteousness is the gradual removal of corruption by the power of Christ and His Spirit. Man is not justified before God by this renewal, neither does he thereby become a child of God, but being already Christ's own, he follows Him and is gradually conformed to His image.

4. Both sermons are characterized by a strong tone of assurance and joy of salvation, which distinguishes them from his earlier lectures and writings — although it was not altogether lacking even in them.

At the time when Luther published these sermons he was also entering upon his second course of lectures on the Psalms. He started his actual lectures at the beginning of 1519. However, he must have begun their preparation soon after he had finished his lectures on Hebrews (March 27, 1518). Since the rather extensive explanation of the first five Psalms was in print by March 22, 1519,[230] he must have started to work on them at the latest in the summer of 1518.

For the simple reason that Psalms 1—22 speak very little of righteousness, Luther did not have an opportunity to dwell upon the subject to any great extent. Of his occasional statements concerning justification, the most important are to be found in his explanation of Ps. 5:9: "Lead me, O Lord, in Thy righteousness, because of my enemies." In the first edition of these lectures, published on March 22, 1519, Luther comments as follows:

"The righteousness of God *(iustitia Dei)* . . . should . . . be understood to mean not that by which God Himself is righteous and by which He judges the ungodly, as is the popular opinion,

---

[230] WA. 5, 5. — In his *Preface* of 1545 Luther says: "In the same year (i. e., 1519) I had already returned to lecture the second time on the Psalms. . . ." These words show that the actual lectures started in 1519.

but, as St. Augustine states in his treatise *On the Spirit and the Letter*, that by which God justifies man, namely, that very mercy or justifying grace by which we are reckoned *(reputamur)* righteous before God. Concerning it the Apostle says in Romans 3: But now apart from the Law the righteousness of God hath been manifested, witnessed by the Law and the Prophets. It is called both the righteousness of God and our righteousness, because it is bestowed upon us by His grace, in the same manner as it is the work of God *(opus Dei)* that operates in us, the Word of God which is spoken to us, the virtue of God which is wrought in us by Him, and so forth. Thus Psalm 30: 'Deliver me in Thy righteousness. . . .' To speak thus concerning the righteousness of Christ — since it differs from the manner of common speech — has caused many people numerous difficulties. Yet we are not to reject altogether the interpretation that the righteousness of God in the above also means the righteousness by which God is righteous, in order that God and we might be righteous by the same righteousness, as by the same word God makes us to be, and we are, what He is, that we may be in Him and His being *(esse)* may be our being. But these things are more sublime than is allowed here and now, and they are uttered in a sense different from that in which they understand it." [231]

The conception of justification as contained in these statements of Luther is in full accord with the evangelical doctrine; the righteousness of God, or of Christ, is bestowed upon the sinful man as a free gift, and thereby he is reckoned or imputed *(reputamur)* righteous before God.

One of the finest expressions of the new insight, and of the assurance of salvation resulting from it, is to be found in Luther's booklet entitled *Fourteen Consolations for Them Who Labor and Are Heavy Laden (Tessaradecas consolatoria pro laborantibus et oneratis)*, written probably in August and September, 1519, for Luther sent the Latin manuscript of it to Spalatin on the 22d of September, 1519.[232] The booklet contains many traditional thoughts, but in the last chapter there is a "song of songs" of justification and salvation in Christ:

"Here there is nothing at all of evil, for Christ, being risen from the dead, dieth no more; death hath no longer dominion over Him. . . . But what is it that He has wrought through His resurrection? He has destroyed sin and brought righteousness to light, abolished death and restored life, conquered hell and bestowed upon us everlasting glory.

"All these are such inestimably precious blessings that the mind of man dare scarcely believe that they have been given to him, as it was with Jacob, who, as it is related in Genesis 45, when he heard that his son Joseph was ruler in Egypt, was like one awakened out of deep slumber. . . .

"This is indeed a most wonderful 'wagon,' that God has made Him unto us as righteousness and sanctification, redemption and wisdom, as the Apostle says in 1 Corinthians 1. I am a sinner, yet I am drawn in His righteousness, which is given me. I have deserved condemnation, but I am set free by His redemption, the 'wagon' in which I sit secure. Thus a Christian, if he but believe, may boast of the merits of Christ and all His blessings as though he had accomplished them all himself. So certainly are they his own that he may even dare to look forward boldly to the judgment of God, unbearable though it be. . . .

"This, then, is the most glorious picture of all, in which we are . . . set down, I say, in the righteousness of Christ, with which He Himself is righteous, because we cling to that righteousness by which He is well pleasing to God, intercedes for us as our Mediator, and gives Himself wholly to be our own as our High Priest and Protector.

"Therefore, as it is impossible that Christ with His righteousness should not please God, so it is impossible that we should not please Him through our faith, which clings to His righteousness. Hence it follows that a Christian is entirely without sin. And even if he has sins, they can in no wise harm, but are forgiven for the sake of the inexhaustible righteousness of Christ which swallows up all sin and on which our faith relies. . . .

"This picture would be sufficient in itself to fill us with such comfort as would not only make it unnecessary for us to grieve over our evils, but also possible for us to glory in our tribulations. In fact, we would scarcely even feel them for the joy that we have in Christ." [233]

Some of the thoughts expressed by Luther in the above we wish to note with especial emphasis. In Christ the believer possesses such exceedingly great treasures that he finds it difficult to believe that they are truly his. The death and resurrection of Christ has delivered him from sin, death, and hell. In himself he deserves condemnation, but through Christ he is forgiven and becomes a glorious son of God. This wonderful salvation which is his is from beginning to end the work and merit of another, namely, Christ. He is "set down amid strange treasures, merited by the labors of another." He is righteous through the righteousness of Christ. He is sanctified through the holiness of Christ. The entire merit of Christ is his, as though it were his own accomplishment. He is altogether without sin, for the inexhaustible righteousness of Christ swallows up his sins. It is a righteousness so abundant and marvelous that all the griefs and tribulations of this present life practically disappear in its wonderful glory.

Something great and decisive had taken place in the spiritual life of Luther and in his understanding of justification. That is quite evident. The fall or early winter of 1518 had brought him to a new phase in his development, to the possession of the Reformation insight into justification. The Augustinian period of his pilgrimage was past. Justification, in its primary meaning, was no longer a process of becoming righteous. Rather it was the immediate appropriation of the righteousness of Christ. True, Luther never surrendered the insight that man never ceases to be a sinner, that the remnants of sin can be removed only gradually, and that for the sake of Christ, God does not impute this sin that remains as guilt; but all this he now saw as part of sanctification rather than justification.

NOTE. Vogelsang found some fragments of Luther's second lecture course on the Psalms from the library of the Vatican and published them in 1940 (*Unbekannte Fragmente aus Luthers zweiter Psalmenvorlesung* 1518). The fragments were probably written in 1518. An interesting question is: What is the relationship between these manuscript fragments and the first volume of the *Commentary on the Psalms,* published in March, 1519? — We take some quotations from these fragments in order to show the conception of justification which is typical of them.

"Behold, every saint is void of righteousness *(iniustus)* and sinful; and yet, because he prays on account of them and hates himself, he is already at the same time righteous and holy. . . . Therefore, until we are wholly cured and made whole (which does not take place in this life), we are always evil, sin all the time, are always vain, always liars; we are righteous and holy only on account of the fact that we here hate and confess it, sighing to Christ through faith, hoping that we finally may become perfect because He is our righteousness, our redemption, our sanctification, and our wisdom" (*op. cit.,* pp. 44 f., Ps. 4:3).

". . . in this life we do not attain righteousness, but we reach forth unto it and beseech and ask all the time to be justified *(extendimus et quaerimus ac petimus semper iustificari),* to have our debt forgiven. This is the wonderful will of God in his saints, because they are at the same time righteous, because they ask to be justified, and at the same time unjust, because they are to be justified . . . knowingly *(scienter)* sinful, unknowingly *(ignoranter)* holy, or sinful in reality, righteous in hope. . . . As they confess the sin and ask for righteousness, God does not impute sin to them any more. . . . Because of that righteousness which they ask for and which they have not yet apprehended . . . in order to show how great is His mercy, . . . as He accounts us as righteous, although we do not have the righteousness, but only ask for it. Thus, sin and the lack of righteousness remain in us, and yet, sin is not sin and unrighteousness not unrighteousness, because the imputation of the merciful God accepts our request for righteousness. We are thus righteous through an external righteousness *(extrinseca iustitia iusti sumus),* but we are unrighteous through an internal unrighteousness; externally righteous, internally sinful; unrighteous with regard to our life and actions, but righteous through the imputation of God alone" (*ibid.,* pp. 85 f., Ps. 5:12).

Luther explains the words "God of my righteousness" (Ps. 4:11) as follows:

"Oh, what a humble word and acceptable to God! He says, I am not my own righteousness, but God's righteousness or the righteousness out of God.

Our study of Luther's accounts of his spiritual and theological development has revealed that it was the Reformation conception of justification that Luther discovered in the tower of the Wittenberg monastery, and not the Augustinian-Catholic view, which he had known all along. Further investigation has made it evident that this evangelical insight appears for the first time in the writings of Luther during the autumn and winter of 1518–19. The only possible conclusion is that his dating of this discovery in his *Preface* of 1545 is correct.

For the sake of more light upon the matter we shall reconsider the writings of Luther from the autumn and winter of 1518–19.[234] We gather the following observations:

I confess that I am a sinner, but I have righteousness out of Thy liberality. . . . God . . . is my righteousness or the Author, Creator, and Worker of my righteousness, and so my righteousness is not mine, but it is mine out of Thy grace" (*ibid.*, pp. 32 f.).

The conception of justification which we find in these statements belongs to the pre-reformation type, or the same as is found in Luther's early lectures on the Psalms, Romans, and in his explanation of the Penitential Psalms.

In the explanation of Ps. 5:8, where we have found a clear reference to the "tower experience" in the printed text, there is no such statement in these fragments. Luther only says:

"Lead me, O Lord, in Thy righteousness, which is God's righteousness, which is of Thee through grace, not in my own or my human one, as those ungodly people assume . . ." (*ibid.*, p. 64).

It is apparent that Luther had not had his tower experience when he wrote these explanations to the first Psalms. Thus, it is evident that *his discovery of the Gospel took place during the time when he was preparing his lectures on the Psalms.* It was for this very reason that he wrote anew these parts of his explanations. His insight into justification had changed, and he wrote his references to his discovery of the evangelical insight into justification in his rewritten draft of the Commentary.

Although Vogelsang does not date the tower experience to this time, he makes the observation that a quite notable development had occurred in Luther's conception of justification and of Christianity in general in the time between the writing of these fragments and the publication of the final commentary (*ibid.*, pp. 24 ff.).

[234] We purposely omit Luther's "shorter" *Commentary on Galatians*, though,

1. In his *Commentary on the Psalms*, Luther remarks that the phrase "the righteousness of God" has caused difficulties to many, because it differs from the ordinary manner of speech. He does not speak at this point in the first person, but undoubtedly he has in mind difficulties which he himself had but recently overcome.

2. Luther states in his second course on the Psalms that his interpretation of the righteousness of God conflicts with the understanding of others *(alio sensu dicta quam illi sentiunt)*. This statement is evidence to the fact that in 1519 he was aware of his disagreement with the Roman Church on this particular point. His lectures of 1513—15, or even of 1516—18, reveal no such consciousness of dissension. That was hardly possible, since his understanding of the phrase "the righteousness of God" was also that of the others.

3. *The Commentary of the Psalms*, 1519, contains a reference to Augustine, according to which Luther believes that in his treatise *On the Spirit and the Letter*, this church father explains the phrase "the righteousness of God" in the same manner as he now does. — According to his *Preface* of 1545, Luther discovered after his tower experience that also Augustine interpreted this phrase to mean that righteousness with which God endows man in justification.

4. In the same manner as in his *Preface*, Luther declares in his

---

in part at least, it belongs to this same period. This commentary was originally written in 1516—17, given to the printer in the fall of 1518 with the hope that it would be published by the winter of 1519. It was, however, recalled by Luther after his negotiations with Miltitz and revised to an extent, and returned to the printer in April, 1519. The revision was by no means thorough. Even the new edition of 1523 was altered but slightly (WA. 2, 436 f.). It is to be expected, therefore, that with the exception of a few later insertions here and there the "old" view prevails in this commentary. Luther himself, conscious of its weaknesses, remarked later: "I did not think that my first commentary on Galatians was so poor. Oh! It is of little use today, it was but my first contention against confidence in works" (WA. 40, 1, 2).

lectures in 1519 that the terms "the work of God," "the virtue of God," and others are analogous to the phrase "the righteousness of God," and also names for faith in Christ.

5. In both cases, in his statements of 1518—19 and in his *Preface* of 1545, Luther asserts that "the righteousness of God" is the imputed righteousness of Christ, revealed in the Gospel and bestowed upon the sinner as a free gift.

The agreement between Luther's two accounts of his discovery, which, although separated by twenty-six years, are almost identical, indicates that this decisive event in his life was preserved quite accurately in his memory. This fact is an effective refutation of the assumption of Boehmer and others that Luther failed to remember correctly the most decisive incidents of his life, badly confusing them as to their dates and content.

Perhaps Luther could have been more accurate and gone into greater detail in describing the exact nature and content of the new insight. However, it is quite understandable that he considered such an explanation unnecessary. All who read his *Preface* — even the Roman Catholics who at Trent declared Luther's doctrine anathema — were thoroughly familiar with his new conception of righteousness and justification. How could he forsee that some "scholars" would suppose that it was the Augustinian-Roman Catholic conception of justification that he discovered, being unable to recognize in his statements a reference to the doctrine which he had so clearly taught for twenty-six years?

At yet another point the statements in the *Preface* of 1545 are in full agreement with facts. Luther declares that already before his discovery of the evangelical conception of justification he knew something of the Scriptural way of salvation, having already "eaten the first fruits of the knowledge of Christ and faith in Him." Therefore, the experience in the tower of the Wittenberg monastery was not at all initial in his spiritual and theological development. On the contrary, it was a kind of culmination or conclusion. The light of the Gospel had reached his heart with its first rays through the instrumentality of Staupitz. Furthermore, as Luther relates in his *Preface* of 1545, by the time of his tower experience he was free from the error of obvious work-righteousness. He already understood "that we are justified and saved not through works, but through faith in Christ." All his lectures and other writings which date from 1513 to 1518 agree in their testimony to this fact. During this same period Luther left behind many of the errors of the Roman Church, although he had not yet received the full light on the doctrine of justification. "One little word" — "the righteousness of God" *(iustitia Dei)* — deprived him of full understanding at this point *(obstiterat hactenus . . . unicum vocabulum).* This word was the key to the full evangelical insight into justication. When Luther found this "key," he entered into the "Paradise" of full evangelical faith.

This statement of Luther concerning the "one little word" which barred his way indicates that prior to his tower experience there were conflicting elements in his faith and theology. On the one hand, he believed in Christ as his Savior; he knew God as the Father who loved sinners and sent His Son to suffer and die for their salvation; he believed in the forgiveness of sins in Christ and His redemptive blood, as it was proclaimed in the Gospel and personally applied in the absolution. On the other hand, there was this "little word," "the righteousness of God," which troubled him, because he understood it as an expression of the retributory justice of God. This conception was concealed in the Augustinian-Catholic doctrine of justification, according to which man must become righteous and sinless in the whole of his life and being in order to be able to stand in the judgment of Christ.

Thus there were actually two conceptions of salvation simultaneously striving for superiority in the soul of Luther: (1) a personal faith in the grace and forgiveness of God in Christ; (2) the view that God requires perfect obedience of heart and life of those who are to be saved. This latter conception, even in its Augustinian form, destroyed to an extent the peace and confidence

Luther's "Tower Experience" 107

he had found through the help of Staupitz. The tower experience served to remove this obstacle and conflict, with the result that he found peace in a full and consistent evangelical faith. Now he realized that man is justified "passively" by the unmerited gracious imputation of God, and that the righteousness thus bestowed is appropriated by faith from the promise of the Gospel.[235]

We now turn to consider the problem of the date of the tower experience.

After his remarks about the Leipzig disputation with Johann Eck, his negotiations with Karl von Miltitz, and the miserable end of Tetzel — all of which occurred during the first half or middle of 1519 — Luther goes on to say:

"Meanwhile, the same year, I had returned to the exposition of the Psalter, confident that after the academic treatment of the Letters of St. Paul to the Romans and Galatians and the Epistle to the Hebrews I was better trained. But I had been possessed with an unusually ardent desire to understand Paul. . . ."

Following his account of the discovery, Luther continues: "Better equipped by these considerations, I began to expound the Psalms the second time. . . ."

On the basis of these statements the following facts are evident:

1. Luther does not confuse his first and second lectures on the Psalms. He clearly distinguishes them by saying twice that this was his second course on the Psalter.

---

[235] J. v. Walter, *op. cit.*, pp. 416 f., correctly states that Luther's words in the *Preface* make it evident that already before his tower experience he had approached the final understanding of the Pauline Gospel. His statement that he had expounded the Scriptures for many years shows that he possessed justifying faith as early as 1512, though he yet lacked the full Reformation doctrine of justification.

Von Walter is right also when he says that Luther's discovery was not the birth of justifying faith in his soul, but rather the revelation of the Reformation doctrine of justification and of its exegetical foundation. — Von Walter, nevertheless, believes that Luther's discovery took place in 1512, and that, in establishing its date in his *Preface* of 1545, he made a mistake of six years.

2. He began his second course on the Psalms in the same year in which he had his negotiations with von Miltitz and the disputation at Leipzig (end of June and beginning of July, 1519) and in which the miserable end of Tetzel occurred. The use of the pluperfect *redieram*, "had returned," shows that the beginning of these lectures took place prior to the above events, that is, in the beginning of the year 1519.

3. The second pluperfect "I had been possessed" *(captus fueram)* indicates that the phrase "the righteousness of God" had troubled him prior to his lectures on the Psalter. The statement that he entered upon this course of lectures "better equipped by these considerations" shows that he started his lectures after his discovery.

4. Luther's search for the true meaning of the words of Paul in Rom. 1:17 transpired between his lectures on Hebrews (completed on March 27, 1518) and the second course on the Psalter. The second pluperfect, "had been possessed," refers to the time prior to the lectures on the Psalms but subsequent to the lectures on Hebrews, previously mentioned. The double pluperfect is in this case the only proper use of tenses.

5. The evangelical insight into justification is not found in the manuscript fragments which Luther wrote in 1518 while preparing his second course of lectures on the Psalms, neither do they have any reference to his tower experience. But the printed *Commentary on the Psalms* has a clear expression of the new insight and a reference to his discovery of it. Our conclusion is that Luther's tower experience took place during the time he was preparing his second course of lectures on the Psalms, probably in the autumn or early winter of 1518. After his discovery he rewrote some parts of his manuscript.

Thus we have been able to establish the date of Luther's discovery of the evangelical insight into justification from the testimony of two sets of documents: (1) From the direct references of Luther in his *Preface* of 1545 and his statements in his table talks, and (2) from the fact that his Reformation conception of justification appears the first time in his writings in the autumn and winter of 1518—19. The testimony of each of these sets of documents is quite conclusive in itself. The fact that both of them point to the same date makes the result doubly reliable.

There are, however, certain difficulties which require solution. The most serious of them results from the fact that Luther had read Augustine's treatise *On the Spirit and the Letter* before the year 1518. But in his *Preface* of 1545 he writes:

"Afterwards I read Augustine's treatise *On the Spirit and the Letter*, where, contrary to my expectation, I found that he also interprets the righteousness of God in a similar way. God endows us with righteousness when He justifies us. And although he explained it imperfectly and did not expound clearly everything concerning imputation, nevertheless he seemed to teach the righteousness of God by which we are justified."

The understanding prevailing in Luther research is that since Luther quoted this treatise in his lectures on Romans (1515), recommended it to Spalatin in 1516, and furthermore published it in 1518 with a preface of his own, his meaning must be that this discovery occurred before Easter, 1515, or prior to the beginning of his lectures on Romans.

This conception rests on the supposition that what Luther intended to say was that after his discovery he read this treatise for the first time. To be sure, at the first glance the words seem to mean just that. However, the first glance often leads astray. In order to understand the statement, we must study the context and the circumstances of the writing.

It is an established fact that Luther did not read the treatise *On the Spirit and the Letter* for the first time in 1514—15. Since he refers to it several times in his marginal notes to Lombard,[236] he must have read it as early as 1509. If the meaning of Luther in his *Preface* of 1545 is construed to be that he read this booklet for the first time after his tower experience, we are faced with the same difficulty, even if we assume that this experience took place in 1512–13.[237]

The clue to the right understanding of the intended meaning of Luther is to be found in the words "contrary to expectation." Luther expected to find something very definite when he opened the booklet again. It is very probable that his expectations were based on his earlier study of the treatise. Not yet possessing the evangelical interpretation of the "the righteousness of God," he found his "old" conception in this booklet. For the simple reason that he was so well acquainted with the treatise and was accustomed to read it with his "old eyes," he expected to discover the old view when he read it again. Very likely he also cherished some hope of finding in it confirmation for his new understanding, since he esteemed Augustine as one of the best teachers of the Church. And so it happened that Augustine seemed to explain the phrase "the righteousness of God" in agreement with his new understanding — though not clearly, especially in the matter of imputation.

If a person who possesses the evangelical conception of justification reads this booklet today — particularly the statements on "the righteousness of God" — the impression is pretty much the same. Perhaps he does not expect to find the right interpretation, but it seems that Augustine explains the phrase "the righteousness of God" in agreement with Luther, even though he does not do it "clearly and perfectly." In reality, of course, Augustine means the "sanative" justification, but somehow his words suggest the evangelical interpretation. The same deceptive quality is characteristic of some of the statements of Luther himself which date from the years when he still held his pre-Reformation views. Taken out of their context they appear to suggest his later doctrine, but

---

[237] Hamel, *op. cit.*, II, 110, suggests that Luther probably had forgotten that he had read this booklet, because it had made no impression upon him. Such an explanation can be used only as a last resort.

Luther's "Tower Experience"   111

in their context they actually contain his pre-Reformation conception.

It is a rather common thing that when a new light of faith and salvation has dawned into the heart of men, books that have been formerly read are seen with "new eyes" and in a new light, even though they may speak "imperfectly" of the new understanding of salvation. After his discovery of the true interpretation of Rom. 1:17 Luther saw many passages of Scripture in an entirely new light. The same must be said of Augustine's treatise *On the Spirit and the Letter*.

This interpretation, the only reasonable one, makes it possible to accept the words of Luther as they are, assuming only such things as are psychologically quite common and understandable.[238]

---

[238] Some scholars, unwilling to assume that Luther erred in his account of the date of his discovery, have sought to interpret his words as referring to the time prior to his first lectures on the Psalms or at least before his lectures on Romans.

Ernst Stracke has made a special study of this question (*Luthers grosses Selbstzeugnis 1545*, Leipzig, 1926). He shows correctly that Luther's use of the double pluperfect refers to the time prior to the beginning of his lectures on the Psalter in 1519. But he denies that the other limit is the course on Hebrews. He holds that the reference to the reading of Augustine's treatise *On the Spirit and the Letter* places it before the Easter of 1515 (pp. 122 ff.).

A year prior to the publication of Stracke's book J. Mackinnon presented a similar interpretation in his *op. cit.*, I, p. 149. According to Mackinnon, Luther does not mean to say in his *Preface* that "the discovery took place in the year in which he returned to the exposition of the Psalms, i. e., 1519. The mention of this second exposition carries his mind back to his previous courses on the Pauline Epistles, and this again recalls the difficulty he had once experienced in understanding Paul, which evidently lay still farther back. What he says on this subject is evidently a reminiscent of parenthesis which refers not to the year 1519, in which he began his second course on the Psalms, but to the absorbing quest for the true meaning of the passage in Romans 1, which preceded not only it, but his previous courses on the Epistles and the Psalms. He is not concerned to give the exact date of the discovery in which this quest ended, and merely adds that, by this discovery and his subsequent experience as an exegete, he was better fitted to expound the Psalms."

This interpretation of Mackinnon expresses in all essential points also the

There remains yet another difficulty. In painting a picture of his spiritual condition prior to his discovery, Luther used very dark colors. It might be argued, therefore, that this picture does not correspond with his state of affairs in 1518, but fits rather the circumstances of 1512. Luther writes concerning himself as follows:

"I felt that I was a sinner before God. My conscience was very restless, and I could not trust Him to be propitiated by my satisfactions. I did not love but actually hated that righteous God who punishes sinners. . . ."

Furthermore, he states that his understanding of the phrase "the righteousness of God" was a philosophical one, namely, that it is the active righteousness of God, by which God is righteous and punishes sinners and the unjust.

Must we assume, therefore, that Luther is guilty of error in memory? Not necessarily; we need only to understand his development and his words in their proper perspective. Boehmer makes the observation that it is an "old psychological experience that with men of strong blood the recollection of their struggles, fears, and disillusionments is much more vivid than that of the more pleasant moments which are never entirely lacking even in the most wretched and distressful existence." [239] On the basis of this psychological "rule" it would be quite natural for Luther to pay particular attention to the dark and distressful periods of his life in the monastery. Undoubtedly, because of his conception of the "active" righteousness of God, he experienced the kind of struggles he described in 1545.

There is yet another, a third, fact that we must consider in this connection. We have seen that the development of Luther's teach-

---

conception of Hirsch, *op. cit.*, p. 165; R. Seeberg, *op. cit.*, p. 69; O. Clemen, WA. 54, 177, and 185; and many others. — We believe that J. von Walter is right in saying that the words "but had been hindered . . . by the unique word" *(sed obstiterat hactenus . . . unicum vocabulum),* which refer to the previous phrase "in that year" *(eo anno),* "make it impossible to understand the account of the discovery as a kind of parenthesis."

ing of justification was closely connected with the deepening of his conception of sin. As early as 1513—15, during his first lecture course, he realized that even the good works of Christians, though effected by the Holy Spirit, are not flawless, but need the grace of God to "cover" their sinfulness.

Gradually the insight of Luther into sin and the accompanying depravity of man became more radical and profound. The good deeds performed by believers are not only imperfect and soiled by unclean motives; they are actually mortal sins in themselves acceptable to God solely for the sake of Christ.

Luther's conception of repentance, as it is revealed in his first series of lectures on the Psalms, was slightly colored with the idea of merit. Self-condemnation and "justification of God" were understood to make man somewhat worthy of grace. This last human "merit" or "disposition" was not surrendered even in the lectures on Romans. Then came the day when Luther perceived and realized the meaning of the Word of God that man is totally sinful and depraved. He saw that he could in no way prepare himself for, or become worthy of, grace. Even as a Christian, his "active" righteousness was but "filthy rags."[240] His sanctification was no longer a satisfactory and secure foundation on which to stand before God. The thought that in the final judgment of God his case depended somewhat on his progress in holiness became more and more unbearable to him. His feeling was that then he had but little hope of eternal life.[241]

---

[241] L. Pinomaa, *Der existentielle Character der Theologie Luthers* (Helsinki, 1940), pp. 19—142 (summary, pp. 136—142), points out how Luther's conception of the Christian faith became more and more a matter on which his whole existence, his life and death, depended. His confidence in his own possibilities disappeared. This was true in regard to several aspects or phases of his faith and theology. He rejected the doctrine of synteresis and understood the conscience to be the judging and accusing "voice" in man whereby he experiences the judgment and wrath of God. Fear ceased to be a meritorious disposition in man and became a terror and trembling before God on account of sin. In affliction the confidence of man in himself and his own

True, Luther was aware of the fact that exegetes in general interpreted the righteousness of God as His grace. But his difficulties were caused by "the common manner of speech among men" and the "philosophical" interpretations of this phrase found frequently in the medieval dogmatic theologians. This fact, together with the deepened insight into sin, gave rise to the crisis spoken of in the *Preface* of 1545. It was nothing unusual for him to see his secret self-righteousness and wrong conception of "the righteousness of God" in a form somewhat exaggerated. That is the common experience of all Christians; their "darkness" preceding their conversion appears much more dense to them than to an uninvolved observer. Had Luther been an exception to this psychological "rule," he would not have been a true man.

We must conclude, therefore, that for lack of sufficient testimony to the contrary we cannot doubt that Luther related facts when he spoke of the trouble and anguish of conscience which he experienced before his discovery in the tower. Else the discovery would not have affected his spiritual life in such a profound way. The

---

possibilities is entirely shattered, and hope in the divine mercy is all that remains. The thought of the possibility of man to fulfill the Law of God was replaced by the insight that the Law serves simply to reveal sin and to bring man into anguish because of sin and the just wrath of God. Humility ceased to be an achievement of man whereby he disposes himself for grace and became a terror of conscience produced by the revelation of divine demands and divine wrath in the Law. Thus Luther's insight into the sin of man and his resultant predicament was profoundly deepened. In certain respects this development reached a kind of climax already during the lectures on Romans, but in the matter of humility the old view prevailed — with an admixture of new ideas — until 1518. — We find ourselves in agreement with Pinomaa. Such a deepened insight into sin and the "existential" predicament of man (that is, of Luther himself) brought Luther to the point where the Augustinian conception of justification became unbearable and irreconcilable with the new insights mentioned above. He who sees his sin and helplessness as did Luther in 1518 cannot find peace and security for his soul unless he can believe that he is righteous solely through the atoning work of Christ and its gracious imputation to him.

retributive order of salvation which lay at the bottom of the Augustinian-Catholic doctrine of justification, though in a refined and subtle form, made it difficult for him to apprehend the free salvation promised in the Gospel. As soon as he was freed from the bonds of this order and understood the way of salvation and the free grace of God in a fully evangelical manner, he experienced a wonderful release. In describing his former conception with what may appear as overstatements in his accounts of his discovery, Luther actually brought to light the true nature of the Augustinian-Catholic doctrine of justification, stripped of all its "sheep's-clothing."

Luther scholars in general are of the opinion that the discovery of the evangelical interpretation of Rom. 1:17 and Ps. 31:2 transpired within the framework of the fourfold meaning of Scripture, with the emphasis upon the tropological interpretation.[242]

One may indeed find statements in the first lecture courses of Luther which point in such a direction.

"He who desires to understand properly the Apostle and the other Scriptures must understand them all tropologically. The truth, wisdom, power, salvation, righteousness are, namely, those by which He makes us strong, saved, righteous, wise, etc."[243]

However, in spite of the similarity in the words, his statement contains a conception of "the righteousness of God" and justification different from that which Luther discovered in 1518.

The formula of the fourfold meaning of Scripture played a significant role in the Augustinian-Catholic interpretation of justification. Therefore, not only did it not help, but it actually hindered Luther in his search for the true meaning of the Biblical statements concerning the righteousness of God. Not until after its rejection was it possible to arrive at the new understanding of these statements. In fact, Luther abandoned the *Quadriga* as early as 1516—17,[244] that is, more than a year before his tower experience. In his lectures on the Psalms in 1519—21 he took a definite stand against this manner of interpretation. His sole interest was to find the simple literal sense of the text, which was not identical with the "literal sense" of the *Quadriga*. Rather, it was the "German and proper sense."[245] Many of the passages that he had previously interpreted in their "literal" sense as referring to Christ, he now explained as speaking of David. In other instances the simple literal meaning compelled him to explain the words as pointing to Christ.[246] It was only natural that Luther should now become more interested in grammar and the original text. Previously he had preferred the Vulgate.[247]

Interpreted according to the tropological sense, Christ and His Cross lose their significance as redemption and atonement and become more an example of cross-bearing and humility. Within this framework "the theology of the Cross" *(theologia crucis)* is more a teaching of how God deals with sinners according to the "pattern" of Christ than good news of what Christ had done for them. Consequently, the tropological interpretation practically forced one to understand justification as a renewal, wherein man was lifted up, step by step, from sin to righteousness and conformity to Christ. Thus, instead of helping to understand justification by grace through faith for the sake of Christ in the true Scriptural sense, it made it nearly impossible.

Not until he had rejected the formula of the fourfold meaning of Scripture was Luther free to study the real, literal meaning of the message of the Bible. What he discovered in the tower of the Wittenberg monastery was the literal meaning of the words of Paul. Then for the first time Luther saw into the heart of the Gospel without the spectacles of traditional formulas. He saw that in its literal sense the Bible teaches justification by imputation. This righteousness through forgiveness of sins in the blood of

---

[247] Hahn, *op. cit.*, pp. 199—207. — Hahn says that from 1518 on Luther rejected the methods of exegesis that tried to "give sense" to Scriptural text and cleaved to the simple literal sense (pp. 210, 213 ff.). — Reinhold Seeberg, *op. cit.*, p. 84, agrees.

Christ is appropriated in its totality by faith once for all. Thereby man becomes acceptable and pleasing to God. In its literal sense the Scriptures also teach that Christ is the pattern, exemplar *(Urbild)*, which reveals how God deals with those He saves, since "it is enough for the disciple that he be as his master" (Matt. 10:25). This thought Luther never surrendered. It continued to occupy a place in his general conception of Christianity. To the end of his life he believed that God not only reckons sinners righteous when they believe in His Son; He also makes them righteous and renews them into the image of His Son. The latter activity of God, however, is not an instrinsic element of justification by faith before God, but belongs to the "gifts of grace," or sanctification. In regard to his justification man stands on the rock of Christ's work *for* him and that alone.

Throughout his life Luther taught a "theology of the Cross." However, there is to be found a fundamental difference between his theology of the Cross prior to his tower experience and following it. In the former, the central theme was the Cross that man has to bear in the footsteps of Christ and the way of the Cross which God uses to save His elect. After his experience in the tower Luther began to emphasize as the central theme the Cross of Christ which He bore for the sinner. Consequently his early theology was a theology of humility, characteristic of which were repentance, self-accusation, pleading for mercy. In his maturity he taught a theology of justification the important elements of which were the work of Christ for man, forgiveness of sins, justification by imputation, and grateful joy of salvation.[248]

---

[248] Thimme, *op. cit.*, pp. 19—30, 59 ff., 161 ff., presents well the differences between Luther's earlier and later teachings. In the lectures on Romans and Hebrews, Luther considered Christ as an example or, rather, pattern, *Urbild*. The work of God in man was then the center of his theology. In the larger *Commentary on Galatians* (1531—35) and in the later disputations this idea gave way to the atoning work of Christ, which became the central factor in justification. In his later lectures and writings Luther earnestly warned Christians not to take Christ for an example in justification. Christ as an example is to be left to the "second righteousness," or the fruits of faith.

When Luther rejected the tropological interpretation of Scripture (and the *Quadriga* in general), he did not surrender all the thoughts associated with it, for most of them rested on a Biblical foundation. The error of the Roman Catholic theology consisted in setting these various elements in wrong order and false relationship to one another. Not the words of Scripture itself, but the traditional doctrine of the Church determined the understanding of the Pauline statements concerning justification. The discovery in the tower gave Luther an insight into the true meaning of Scripture, enabling him to bring order into the Christian faith and doctrine.

The change which took place in Luther's attitude toward Mysticism by the year 1519 is further evidence of a crisis having occurred in his spiritual life and theology at that time. During his lectures on Romans in 1515—16 he believed that the German Mystics possessed the same conception of salvation as he — and this assumption was not altogether false. In 1518 Luther published the *German Theology* and gave it his hearty recommendation. But the influence of German Mysticism upon him came to an end about 1518—20. This is a fact well established by modern Luther research.[249] And it was more than coincidence. It was impossible

---

[249] Quiring, *op. cit.*, p. 222, states: "The influence of medieval Mysticism on Luther can be shown until about 1518—20; then it ceases, except at the points where this Mysticism helped him forward. . . . Therefore it can be held that this development comes to its end with the year 1520. . . . It is remarkable that at this time the *German Theology* disappears from the lecture catalogue of Wittenberg."

Vogelsang, "Luther und Mystik," *op. cit.*, pp. 34 f., shows that Luther criticized Areopagite as early as 1516; but in 1519—20 he rejected him altogether, saying that he was "wholly detrimental, more Platonic than Christian. . . . You will not learn to know Christ there. . . . I know it from experience" (WA. 5, 165;17). — Already H. Hering, *Die Mystik Luthers* (Leipzig, 1879), p. 292, came to the conclusion that from the year 1519 on specifically mystical thoughts began to disappear from Luther's understanding of the Christian faith and way of salvation.

Luther's "Tower Experience"

for Luther to be freed from Mysticism as long as he did not possess the Reformation doctrine of justification and its relation to sanctification, or the true distinction between the Law and the Gospel. Upon his arrival at the right understanding of these doctrines in his tower experience the mystical ideas concerning salvation fell away as dead leaves from an oak tree in the spring, when new life brings forth new living leaves. It is quite impossible to assume — as many Luther students do — that Luther preserved for about six years mystical and other Catholic views alongside his new evangelical faith. In reality they disappeared immediately after the dawn of the new evangelical light of justification in his heart.[250]

---

[250] Grisar, *Luther* I, 399, avers that Luther's great problem which found its solution in the tower experience was this: "How is the imputed justice of God to become mine? Not by yearning prayer and other works which hitherto he had proposed as the means, but by faith only which has assured him of regeneration, of heavenly revelations. . . ."

This statement of Grisar has two misunderstandings. First, Luther's problem was not how to appropriate the imputed righteousness. Rather, was "the righteousness of God" to be understood as a renewal in man, or was it a bestowal of the Christ-merited righteousness upon the sinner through God's gracious imputation? Secondly, Luther did not receive certainty of justification through any "assurance of regeneration and heavenly revelations," but through faith in the promise of the Gospel. An "assurance of regeneration," that is, of the change which has taken place in man — if this is what Grisar means — belonged to the "old" Augustinian-Catholic conception of justification, and not to the Lutheran. An "assurance of heavenly revelations" also belonged to the "old" Romish religiosity, in which "heavenly revelations" have been some of the strongest supports of unscriptural doctrine; it was also part and parcel of the mystical and "fanatic" *(schwaermerisch)* sectarian piety, against which Luther fought throughout his life. Grisar goes to the extreme in misunderstanding Luther's discovery at this particular point. Luther repeatedly warned Christians against reliance upon any experiences and "heavenly revelations" above or beside the Word of God, for they could be delusions of the devil or illusions of one's own mind. The Christian should cling to the Word and Sacraments, in which God promises and imparts His justifying grace.

Grisar asserts that at the time of his discovery Luther "transformed the faith necessary for justification into a mere act of confidence in the merits of Christ without any reference to the Sacraments, the other truths of faith, or the Church, the guardian and mouthpiece of faith" (*ibid.*, p. 385).

Anyone acquainted with the teachings of Luther knows that he never taught a confidence in the merits of Christ without reference to the Sacraments, the Church, and the other truths of faith. On the contrary, he connected it inseparably with these. Throughout his life Luther fought against the "fanatics" (*Schwarmgeister*) who did that of which Grisar accuses him. H. E. Weber, *Reformation, Orthodoxie und Rationalismus* (Guetersloh, 1939), pp. 2 f., says in a sweeping statement, which, however, can be correctly understood, that "not only the Catholics know that forgiveness is to be found in the Church alone. Such a foolish individualism which does not perceive this is, at any rate, foreign to the Reformation."

Summary and Conclusion

AFTER his entrance into the monastery, Luther experienced two great crises. The first was his conversion, or his coming to a personal faith in the forgiveness of sins in Christ. This occurred in the year 1512, probably toward the end of October or in November. The central issue in this crisis was how to attain the certainty of the forgiveness of God, that is, how to be assured that God truly forgave his sins when absolution was proclaimed to him. His false conception of repentance, absolution, and predestination were great obstacles in his path at this point. A further stumbling block was the traditional unevangelical form of absolution which was in use in the monastic order. Through the counsels of Staupitz, Luther gained the right understanding of these questions, and so was able to appropriate the assurance of forgiveness of sins pronounced by Staupitz. And so "the light of the Gospel began to shine" into his heart, and he "ate the first fruits of faith and the knowledge of Christ," as he later related. Inseparably associated with the influence of Staupitz was that of Augustine, Bernhard, and Mysticism. Staupitz himself was greatly influenced by these.

Though Luther possessed a saving faith already in 1512, his conception of justification was not that of his mature period. He understood justification as a gradual process of religious and moral renewal, or healing of the human nature from the corruption of sin. Non-imputation of sins, that is, non-reckoning of sins that remain, for the sake of Christ, was but a temporary supplement to this process of healing. True, Luther at times said, following Augustine, that this non-imputation formed the greater portion of justification, since the actual righteousness of the believer was a mere beginning in this earthly life.

This time, between the late fall of 1512 and the summer of 1518, may well be termed the twilight period of the Reformation. The first rays of the sun of grace and righteousness were already lighting the sky in Luther's spiritual life, but the actual daybreak had not yet taken place. The full light of the evangelical insight into justification had not yet reached his soul. The light which he did possess, however, was nearly sufficient to break the bonds of the Roman Church, as had been the case also with Wycliffe and Huss, who had about as much revealed to them as Luther at this particular time, but who did not know the evangelical doctrine of justification. In his struggles against the abuses within the Church, Luther at this time directed his efforts toward removal of errors in the sphere of doctrines in which he had already or almost attained the evangelical insight, principally the doctrine of repentance.

The second great crisis, the actual daybreak, in Luther's development, was his tower experience toward the end of the year 1518. It resulted or consisted in his discovery of the evangelical or Reformation insight into justification. Two groups of historical documents give evidence of this great change: (1) Luther's *Preface* to his works, written in 1545, and scattered statements in his table talks of different dates; (2) Luther's lectures and writings. The first group of documents contains accounts of the nature and date of this discovery from the pen and mouth of Luther himself. The second group yields information concerning Luther's conception of justification in the early period of his life. Both in their own way testify irrefutably to the fact that Luther discovered his Reformation concept of justification toward the end of the year 1518. It is this year that marks the beginning of the Reformation movement in the deepest meaning of the word, with its watchword of justification by the gracious imputation of God appropriated through faith. This watchword was unknown prior to year 1519. Closely connected with the discovery of the true meaning of Rom. 1:17, as a kind of prerequisite, was the rejection of the fourfold meaning of Scripture and, as its inevitable consequence, the surrender of Mysticism.

Summary and Conclusion

The discovery in the tower, however, did not result in Luther's casting overboard his old views one and all. This was impossible since many of his pre-Reformation conceptions were perfectly Scriptural. To the very end he continued to teach that grace is bestowed only upon the humble and contrite in heart, that also the justified children of God are sinful in themselves, that therefore their struggle against sin and gradual mortification of the flesh must never cease in this present life. These beliefs, together with the conviction that man is dependent entirely upon the grace of God for salvation, belonged to the fundamental insights of Luther throughout his life. To the very end he agreed with Augustine in the interpretation of Romans 7, and of a similar passage in Gal. 5:16 ff., namely, that Paul speaks in them primarily as a believer. Consequently, many of the statements in the earlier and later writings of Luther are similar or almost so.

The basic difference between Luther's pre-Reformation and his Reformation doctrine of salvation is to be found in the conception of the nature and essence of justification. The tower experience opened his eyes to see that according to Scripture, and Paul in particular, justification by faith is not a gradual process of renewal or becoming righteous. It is rather the bestowal of the righteousness of Christ by imputation. God justifies the sinner by forgiving his sins and reckoning him innocent and blameless for the sake of the atoning work of Christ. This acquittal God pronounces through the Gospel promises proclaimed by the ministry of reconciliation. By faith the sinner receives this divine gift promised and offered to him. The foundation of justification and also the object of the believer's faith and trust is not what God has done and does *in* him, but what Christ has done *for* him.

In conversion man receives the Holy Spirit, who takes abode in his heart, thereby renewing him in heart and life. This renewal, or sanctification, occurs basically in the new birth and then continues as a process of growth in the knowledge of God and Christ and in holiness of life effected by the operation of the indwelling Spirit.

It was not Luther's conversion or coming to a personal faith that was the primary factor in his becoming the Reformer, although it was a very necessary prerequisite. Only a believer can be a reformer of the Church, but most believers are not reformers. Without his tower experience Luther would have become a "reformist" — like Wycliffe, Huss, Savonarola, and others — but never the Reformer.

Neither was it a mere "religious experience" that made of Luther the Reformer. His task was not to proclaim to the world some sort of new supernatural-mystical revelation. He was more than a prophet of a new religious "idea." Hundreds of false prophets have received their "calling" in this manner, but not Luther.

Luther became the Reformer by discovering the true meaning of the written Word of God, particularly the Word concerning justification. True, his discovery in the tower was also a deep religious experience in which he found peace and joy hitherto unknown to him. But what he felt and experienced was not the central or primary thing. That was the discovery of the Scriptural way of salvation and especially of justification. Never was it the primary purpose of Luther to proclaim religious experiences or ideas. The content of his message was the eternally valid and effective divine truth, revealed by God, recorded in the Scriptures, and preached in the Church. Religious experiences were effects of believing the truth and promise of the Gospel. The entire content of his discovery in the tower was the insight that, according to the simple and literal meaning of this written Word of God, man is justified by the gracious imputation of God when by faith he appropriates the Gospel promise of forgiveness of sins in the blood of Christ.

Luther's discovery of the Reformation insight into justification and sanctification contained both of the principles of the Reformation: (1) that Scripture is the revealed and inspired Word of God and as such is the highest and only standard and norm of Christian faith and life; (2) that according to Scripture the sinner is jus-

Summary and Conclusion 125

tified by grace alone, through faith in Christ, when he trustfully lays hold of the Gospel promise and offer of forgiveness of sins. The former was not the new element in the discovery, but rather its prerequisite. The latter was the new insight that Luther discovered or rediscovered. It was not a new idea, of that Luther was convinced, but the old and original Gospel which the Apostles of Christ had proclaimed but which had been hidden under misconceptions and false doctrine. With this "cover" removed, the central truth of the original faith of the Apostles was again brought to light and began to shine forth, first into the heart of Luther and then through his ministry into the hearts of multitudes from many nations and tongues.[251]

Luther once said, and we quoted his statement earlier in our study, that a volume containing his thoughts of the period prior to his discovery of the full Gospel was of little use in the new era of the noonday Gospel. These words may be applied to the entire literary heritage of the "young Luther." The writings of this period cannot be used alongside the works of the Reformation era. The Lutheran Church has followed the right instinct in owning as its true spiritual possessions only those writings of Luther which date from the year 1519 or later. Almost without exception the instruction in the Church has been based on these, while the writings produced prior to 1519 had been mostly forgotten until the Luther scholars of our own generation brought them to light. The church at large has had the feeling that the earlier works of Luther reflect a different and strange spirit and give expression to an unevangelical conception of the Christian faith and life. Truly "Lutheran" are only the writings after 1518.

Modern Luther research has reversed the stand at this point.

---

[251] Gordon Rupp, *Luther's Progress to the Diet of Worms, 1521* (1951), p. 38, refers to the Finnish edition of the present study, and asserts that the author "divorces Luther's religious problem from his theological research." The exact opposite is the case. Rupp has either had false information of the contents of the present study or has thoroughly misunderstood it.

Many of the studies of Luther's theology fail to distinguish between his earlier and later lectures and writings. On the basis of our study we must regard such a procedure as erring seriously as to method and causing much confusion. Since the literary production of Luther earlier than 1519 is of a pre-Reformation and sub-Reformation type, no sound Luther study can afford to make uncritical use of the writings before and after 1518—19, as though they were in every respect equal. However, a dangerously large part of modern Luther research has committed just this error and is, therefore, in need of thorough revision.[252]

In 1938 Otto Wolff made the statement that as far as the modern study of Luther is concerned the rediscovery of the full Reformation Gospel of the Reformer is still a thing of the future.[253] The Luther research of our day is still living and groping largely in a "pre-Reformation" period. Is it too much to hope that as World War I was followed by a "revival" of the "young Luther," World War II will be followed by a "revival" of the full Reformation Gospel of Luther — and of Scripture?

---

[252] On recent Luther research, Luther's literary heritage, and its literary criticism, see U. Saarnivaara, "Some Questions Concerning Recent Luther Research," *The Lutheran Quarterly*, February 1949, pp. 91 ff. The contents of this article are included in the Introduction of the Finnish edition of the present work.

Notes

1. *On the City of God* (413–426), XIV, 11 f.; *On Nature and Grace* (415), XXV. — *Enchiridion* (421), XXX. The works of Augustine are in J. P. Migne's *Patrologiae cursus completus*. Series Latina (Paris, 1874, 1904), vols. 32–45. The original Latin titles are to be found in the Bibliography.
2. *On Grace and Free Will* (426–427), XXXIII.
3. *On the Spirit and the Letter* (412), IV.
4. *Ibid.*, III.
5. *Ibid.*, XXVII.
6. *On Rebuke and Grace* (426–427), II.
7. On Christian Doctrine (Books I–II: 397, Book IV: 426), I, 25, 27–35.
   Anders Nygren, "Simul iustus und peccator bei Augustin und Luther," *Zeitschrift fuer systematische Theologie*, 1939, pp. 370 ff., presents well the thoughts of Augustine on this issue.
8. *On Nature and Grace* (415), XXI.
9. *On the Spirit and the Letter*, IX. Italics our own.
10. *Ibid.*, X.
11. *Ibid.*, XXVI.
12. *Ibid.*, XVII.
13. *Ibid.*, XXXII.
14. *Ibid.*, XXXVI.
15. Sermo XIX, 2; V, 23; Migne, *op. cit.*, vol. 38, p. 133.
16. Migne, *op. cit.*, vol. 37, p. 1848.
17. Sermo CLIX, Migne, *op. cit.*, vol. 38, p. 868.
18. *Commentary on the Psalms, ibid.*, vol. 37, p. 1825.
19. On Marriage and Concupiscence (419), XXVI.
20. *On the City of God*, XIX, 27.
21. *Enchiridion*, XCIV.
22. *Ibid.*, XCIX.
23. *Den kristna kaerlekstanken genom tiderna. Eros och Agape* II (Stockholm, 1936; translated into English by Philip S. Watson, published by S. P. C. K., London, and Macmillan, New York, under the title *Agape and Eros. A History of the Christian Idea of Love*), pp. 251–274.
24. See footnote.
25. WA. 40, I, 673, 10 (Gal. 4:27).
26. WA. 17, II, 228, 26 (*Church Postil*, 5th Sunday in Lent).

27. WA. 31, II, 439; 18, 772, II (*On the Bondage of the Will*, 1525).
28. WA. 40, I, 235, 15 (Gal. 2:16).
29. WA. 40, I, 48, 1 (Introd. to Gal.)
30. *Ibid.*, p. 444, 13 (Gal. 3:13).
31. WA. 42, 192, 4 (Gen. 4:5).
32. WA. 10, I, 342, 25 (*Church Postil*).
33. WA. Deutsche Bibel, 7, 9, 10 (Preface to Romans, 1522).
34. WA. 39, I, 99, 15 (Disputation of justification, 1536).
35. WA. 39, I, 20 (A disputation, 1536).
35a. WA. 39, I, 380, 2, Disp. against the Antinomians, 1537.
36. *Ibid.*, 434, 4.
37. WA. 39, I, 482, 13 (A disputation, 1538). Cf. pp. 444, 2; 235, 12; 363, 3; 366, 16.
38—42. See footnotes.
43. WA. 1, 525; the same in Enders I, 79.
44. Enders 14, 3107, 31 ff.
45. WA. 43, 461; cf. TR. 5, 5658a.
46. TR. 2, 1490—1532.
47. TR. 2, 1820 — Schlaginhaufen, 1532; cf. TR. 1, 2654a, b.
48. Enders 8, 1731, 35, a letter of consolation to Hieronymus Weller in 1530.
49. *Ibid.*, l. 66.
50. *Ibid.*, l. 32.
51. ". . . tui non decet esse immemores et ingratos; per quem primum coepit evangelii lux de tenebris splendescere in cordibus nostris" (Enders 4, 708, 8).
52. "Sed Staupitius meus dicebat: Man mus den man ansehen, der heyst Christus. Staupitius hat die doctrinam angefangen (TR. 1, 526 — Deitrich, 1533).
53. J. F. Knaake published Staupitz's works in 1867 (*Johannis Staupitii opera*, vol. I, Deutsche Schriften, Potzdam). Henceforth reference to this work will be: "Knaake." As the edition of Knaake has not been available, quotations have been made from Ernst Wolf's work *Staupitz und Luther* (Leipzig, 1927). — G. Buchwald and E. Wolf published in 1927 the early sermons of Staupitz, *Staupitz Tuebinger Predigten* (Leipzig). "Pred." refers to this work.
54. *Ibid.* — Wolf, *op. cit.*, p. 64.
55. *Ibid.*, p. 97.
56. Knaake, p. 102; Wolf, *op. cit.*, pp. 38 ff.
57. Pred., p. 207.
58. *Ibid.*, pp. 128, 132, 196.
59. Knaake, pp. 70 f., 108.

Notes

60. Knaake, pp. 18, 40, 127.
61. Ibid., p. 104.
62. Ibid., p. 17.
63. Ibid., p. 18; Wolf, op. cit., pp. 52 ff.
64. Libellus de executione eternae predestinationis ("LB" according to Wolf's op. cit.)
65. Knaake, p. 102.
66. Pred., p. 95, 5.
67. Knaake, LP. 10.
68, 69. See footnotes.
70. WA. 40, II, 91, 32 (Gal. 5:17) — Philip S. Watson, Let God Be God (London-Philadelphia, Pa., 1948), pp. 15 ff.
71. WA. 40, II, 15, 15 (Gal. 5:3).
72. See footnote.
73. TR. 5, 6017; cf. WA. 21, 291, 34.
74. WA. 40, II, 412.
75. Ibid., Roerer's Hs.
76. WA. 30, II, 449, 1 (On the Keys, 1530).
77. Cf. Gustaf Ljunggren, Synd och skuld i Luthers teologi (Uppsala, 1927), pp. 28 f., Scheel, op. cit., I, 20; II, 263.
78, 79. See footnotes.
80. Wolf, op. cit., pp. 175 ff., Feckes, op. cit., pp. 86 ff.
81. TR. 2, 265a; WA. 5, 170, 10; 622, 24; 209, 36; 2, 638, 9; 56, 182, 14; 386, 6, 24.
82. WA. 56, 401, 9.
83. See footnote.
84. See footnote.
85, 86. See footnotes.
87. WA. 54, 183 f.
88. Ibid., pp. 185 f.
89. TR. 3, 3232 — summer 1532, Cordatus; other versions of the same statement are identical in content.
90. TR. 5, 5247—1540, Mathesius.
91. TR. 5, 5553 — 1542—43, Heydenreych.
92. TR. 5, 5518. Italics our own.
93. H. J. Iwand, Rechtfertigungslehre und Christusglaube (Leipzig, 1930), p. 33, footnote, says: "We think that the dating of the tower experience must remain uncertain as long as it is not clearly determined wherein it consisted in regard to its content."
94. H. Hermelink, "Die neuere Lutherdeutung," Theologische Rundschau, 1935, p. 149, says: "The content (das inhaltliche Element) of the basic

insight of the Reformation needs to be studied more thoroughly than it has been hitherto. This insight needs to be distinguished from the general Christian ideas found in Catholicism *(das Gemeinchristliche im Katholizismus)."*

95. ". . . iustitia Dei, non qua Deus iustus est, sed qua induit hominem; iustitia Dei dicitur, quod impetriendo eam iustos facit; iustitia Dei, non qua ipse iustus est, sed qua nos ab eo iusti facit" (Augustine, *On the Spirit and the Letter*, IX, XI; we have quoted these statements in English before).
96. Migne, *op. cit.*, vol. 17, p. 59B, 79B.
97–105. See footnotes.
106. WA. 9, 17.
107. WA. 9, 42, 36.
108. Occam stated that for his salvation a Christian does not need to know what is not in Scripture or cannot, necessarily and evidently, be concluded from Scripture (*Dialogue*, pp. 411, 769, according to M. Reu, *Luther's German Bible*, Columbus, Ohio, 1934, p. 326).
109. WA. Briefe 1, 174.
110. *Ibid.*, p. 35, 3.
111. *Ibid.*, p. 46, 16.
112. Luther tells of these struggles particularly in his preface to his book *On the Misuse of Masses* (1521), WA. 8, 48 f., and in his *Commentary on Genesis* (1535–45), WA. 42, 301, 31.
113. WA. 9, 59, 32; 60, 1, 7.
114. *Ibid.*, p. 71, 1.
115. *Ibid.*, p. 70, 6.
116. *Ibid.*, p. 72, 10
117. *Ibid.*, p. 72, 27–99, 27.
118. Scheel, *op. cit.* II, 467, and Hamel, *op. cit.* I, 23 ff., say that Augustine and Lombard helped Luther in the matter of expressing the deeper insights he had gained through his struggles in the monastery.
119. TR. 2, 2544a. – Cordatus, 1532.
120. Minor differences exist among the opinions of various scholars in regard to the time when Luther and Staupitz had occasion for mutual intercourse. See, e. g., H. Boehmer, *Der junge Luther* (in English, *Road to Reformation*, translated by Theodore G. Tappert, Philadelphia, Pa., 1946), pp. 100–108; E. Wolf, *op. cit.*, p. 46; Scheel, *op. cit.* II, 369, 346.
121. Cf. Scheel, *op. cit.* I, 550 f.
122. See footnote.
123. See footnote.

Notes

124. See footnote.
125. *Enarrationes in Psalmos*, in Amorbach's edition, 1508.
126–129. See footnotes.
130. WA. 3, 126, 30; 172, 17.
131. *Ibid.*, p. 465, 5 *scholium* Psalm 71/72.
132. *Ibid.*, p. 29.
133. *Ibid.*, p. 429, 9, sch. Ps. 68/69:17.
134. *Ibid.*, p. 433, 28.
135. ". . . et sic humiliati fiunt apti ad misericordiam Dei" (*ibid.*, p. 584, 26, sch. Ps. 77/78:29).
136. See footnote.
137. Sch. Ps. 7:11. Luther found this explanation in Augustine's commentary on the Psalms, Migne, *op. cit.*, vol. 36, p. 104.
138. WA. 3, 91, 10, sch. Ps. 9:16; cf. pp. 76, 32; 84, 3; 94, 4.
139. See footnote.
140. WA. 3, 458, 4.
141. *Ibid.*, p. 465, 1.
142. *Ibid.*, p. 458, 8.
143, 144. See footnotes.
145. Migne, *op. cit.*, vol. 36, p. 877; cf. *Ibid.*, p. 233, Ps. 30/31:2.
146. WA. 3, 231, 37.
147. ". . . semper sumus in motu, semper iustificandi, qui iusti sumus . . . terminus ad quem est iusticia . . ." (WA. 4, 364, 9, sch. Ps. 118/119:122).
148. *Ibid.*, p. 315, 23.
149. E. g., "do not approve his works nor reckon whatever he does for righteousness to him (neque pro iustitia ei reputes), but impute them for iniquity to him" (WA. 3, 458, 21, sch. Ps. 70/71:28).
150. ". . . propter fidem Christi, qui habitat in ipso" (WA. 4, 280, 3). ". . . propter Christum in nobis per fidem" (*ibid.*, p. 408, gl. Ps. 123/124). ". . . propter fidem Christi" (*ibid.*, p. 408).
151. Cf. Vogelsang, *op. cit.*, p. 118. — In the phrase "propter fidem Christi" the genitive *Christi* is an "objective genitive," denoting Christ as the object of faith.
152. WA. 3, 175, 29.
153. ". . . per Christum eis non imputabuntur" (*ibid.*, p. 187, 35).
154. In speaking of the "cross" of a Christian, Luther evidently thought of Christ's words in Mark 8:34; Matt. 10:38; Luke 14:27.
155. WA. 3, 646, 13, sch. Ps. 93/94:4.
156. See footnote.
157. WA. 3, 96, 25, gl. Ps. 11/12:7.

158. Ibid., p. 37, 34, gl. Ps. 4:5.
159. WA. 3, 258, 8.
160. Ibid., p. 368, 18, sch. Ps. 43/44:10.
161. WA. 3, 271, 18.
162. WA. 4, 285, 32.
163. Cf. Hamel, op. cit., I, 169–178.
164. See footnote.
165. J. Mackinnon gives a correct definition of Luther's conception of justification in 1513–17. According to the teaching of Luther during that period, he says, justification "is a process of healing the disease of sin from which the sinner suffers, effecting his moral restoration" (op. cit., p. 203). "Justification thus means for Luther the acquisition of real as well as reputed righteousness. It is the work of God from beginning to end, and only the operation of God's mercy and grace makes it possible. It is the divine method of achieving the regeneration of the believer, and it assuredly realizes God's purpose of which it is alike the vindication and the triumph" (ibid., pp. 210 f.).

Apparently Mackinnon is so under the influence of the Hollian school that he does not see the fundamental difference between Luther's early and mature doctrines of justification.
166. Vogelsang, op. cit., p. 84.
167. Wendorf, op. cit., pp. 304, 320 f.
168, 169. See footnotes.
170. Hamel, op. cit. II, 1 f.
171. Luther wrote of this in his letter to Spalatin on October 19, 1516 (Enders 1, 63), emphasizing that all works done outside of faith in Christ "do not taste of righteousness, any more than rowanberries taste of figs." He noted that most of the church fathers before Augustine explained it like Erasmus.
172. Vogelsang, "Luther und Mystik," *Luther-Jahrbuch*, 1937, p. 32, A. V. Mueller, *Luther und Tauler* (Bern, 1918), and H. Quiring, "Luther und die Mystik," *Zeitschrift fuer systematische Theologie*, 1936, p. 207, differ somewhat on the question whether Luther became acquainted with the "German Mysticism" already toward the end of 1515 or in 1516. – Luther published a part of *German Theology* (the title was given by him) in 1516 and the entire book in 1518. His preface to it is found in WA. 9. – Although the *German Theology (Theologia Deutsch)* was a devotional book, it was at the same time polemical against the radical fanatical movement of the "Brethren of the free spirit" (Brueder des freien Geistes).

Notes

173. Johann Tauler, *Predigten* I–III (Frankfurt a. M., 1826), e. g., Sermons 9, 14, 40, 43, 52, 56. – Cf. Arvid Runestam, *Den kristliga friheten hos Luther och Melanchthon* (Uppsala, 1917), pp. 76–83, and Yrjö J. E. Alanen, *Das Gewissen bei Luther* (Helsinki, 1934), pp. 22 f., 121.
174. See footnote.
175. WA. 56, 177, 14, sch. Rom. 1:20.
176. *Ibid.*, p. 237, 5, sch. Rom. 3:10.
177. *Ibid.*, p. 275, 18, sch. Rom. 4:7.
178. *Ibid.*, p. 355, 28, sch. Rom. 8:3.
179. *Ibid.*, p. 254, 9, sch. Rom. 3:20.
180. *Ibid.*
181. *Ibid.*, p. 214, 13, sch. Rom. 3:14.
182. *Ibid.*, p. 279, 19, sch. Rom. 4:7. ". . . interior iustitia."
183. *Ibid.*, p. 235, 21, sch. Rom. 3:9.
184. *Ibid.*, pp. 256, 29; 264, 5.
185. *Ibid.*, p. 254, 23, sch. Rom. 3:20.
186. *Ibid.*, p. 265, 18, sch. Rom. 3:28.
187. *Ibid.*, p. 271, 11, sch. Rom. 4:7.
188. *Ibid.*, p. 259, 14, sch. Rom. 3:21.
189. *Ibid.*, p. 264, 18.
190. *Ibid.*, p. 260, sch. Rom. 3:21.
191. *Ibid.*, p. 442, 15, sch. Rom. 12. The italics in this and the following quotations are our own.
192. *Ibid.*, p. 254, 29.
193. *Ibid.*, p. 258, 19, sch. Rom. 3:21.
194. *Ibid.*, p. 272, 11, sch. Rom. 4:7.
195. *Ibid.*, p. 272, 8.
196. *Ibid.*, p. 272, 16.
197. *Ibid.*, p. 259, 2.
198. *Ibid.*, p. 269, 21, sch. Rom. 4:9.
199. ". . . in nobis sumus peccatores et tamen reputante Deo iusti per fidem. Quia credimus promittendi, quod nos liberet . . ." (*ibid.*, p. 271, 20).
200. *Ibid.*, p. 347, 8, sch. Rom. 7:25.
201. *Ibid.*, p. 277, 24, sch. Rom. 4:7.
202. *Ibid.*, p. 280, 2.
203. *Ibid.*, p. 278, sch. Rom. 4:7.
204. Rom. 3:20, 28; 4:4; 5:15.
205. See footnote.
206. WA. 56, 318, 20, sch. Rom. 5:15.
207. *Ibid.*, p. 158, 9.
208. *Ibid.*, p. 53, 16, gl. Rom. 5:14.

209. *Ibid.*, p. 97, 24, gl. Rom. 9:33.
210. ". . . sola autem reputante miserentis Dei per fidem eius iusti sumus" (*ibid.*, p. 287, 18, sch. Rom. 4:7).
211. *Ibid.*, p. 27, 26, gl. Rom. 2:13.
212. *Ibid.*, p. 342, 33, sch. Rom. 7:20.
213. Cf. Runestam, *op. cit.*, 56.
214. Hamel, *op. cit.* II, 43—52, gives a good account of Luther's thoughts concerning the Law in these lectures. He does not, however, pay any attention to the difference between them and his mature teaching.
215. See footnote.
216. Johannes Ficker's edition, II, 129, 19, sch. Heb. 2:14, according to Hamel, *op. cit.* II, 137. Cf. Thimme, *op. cit.*, pp. 57, 61.
217. WA. 1, 155.
218. *Ibid.*, p. 167, 7.
219. *Ibid.*, p. 186, 9.
220. *Ibid.*, p. 192, 27.
221. Hamel, *op. cit.* II, 144.
222. This statement is found almost literally also in Luther's *Church Postil*, 2d Sunday in Advent, Epistle sermon, WA. 10, 1, 2, 69, 19. Anders Nygren uses it as the motto of his *op. cit.*
223. WA. 1, 360—365.
224. See footnote.
225. WA. 2, 41 ff.
226, 227. See footnotes.
228. WA. 2, 144 ff.
229. Prior to his statements on the second righteousness Luther says: "And so day by day Christ drives out Adam more and more, according to the growth of faith and the knowledge of Christ. For it is not infused wholly at once, but it begins, proceeds, and is finally perfected through death." This statement apparently belongs to the following paragraph, for just a moment before Luther says that the righteousness of Christ swallows up sin immediately and that the believer already possesses the righteousness of Christ. — Such "jumps" are not uncommon in Luther's writings.
230. See footnote.
231. WA. 5, 144, 1 ff.
232. WA. 6, 99. — The booklet was published in Latin and German at the beginning of February, 1520.
233. WA. 6, 132 ff.
234, 235. See footnotes.
236. WA. 9, 54, 34; 60, 26; 82, 27.

Notes

237. See footnote.
238. See footnote.
239. *Ibid.*, pp. 47 f.
240. In the years 1518–21 Luther treated this question repeatedly, e. g., WA. 2, 44 (1518); WA. 2, 411, 1 (1519); WA. 7, 433 ff. (1520–21).
241. See footnote.
242. So Em. Hirsch, *op. cit.*, pp. 167 f.; E. Vogelsang, *op. cit.*, pp. 22 ff.; A. Hamel, *op. cit.* I, 34 f.; O. Scheel, *op. cit.* II, 595; Erich Seeberg, *Luthers Theologie* II, *Christus Bild und Urbild* (Stuttgart, 1937), pp. 10 f.; E. Sormunen, *op. cit.* II, 49 f.; Rupp, *op. cit.*, p. 38; Schwiebert, *op. cit.*, pp. 283 ff.
243. WA. 3, 458, 8.
244. WA. 1, 507.
245. ". . . germanus et proprius sensus," cf. WA. 5, 75, 22; 122.
246. Cf. WA. 5, 587 f., 595, 14.
247–251. See footnotes.
252. See footnote.
253. Otto Wolff. *Die Haupttypen der neueren Lutherdeutung* (Stuttgart-Berlin, 1938), p. 396: "Diese volle Erneuerung Luthers steht gewiss noch aus."

Bibliography

I. Works of Luther

D. Martin Luthers *Werke*. Kritische Gesamtausgabe. Edited by J. K. F. Knaake, G. Kawerau, etc. (Weimar, 1883 ff.) Commonly known as the "Weimar edition," *Weimarer Ausgabe* (usually referred to with the abbreviation "WA." or with mere numbers).
—, *Saemtliche Werke*. (Erlangen, 1826–57.) *"Erlanger Ausgabe"* ("EA.").
—, *Tischreden*, 6 volumes. (Weimar, 1912–21.) ("TR.").
—, *Briefwechsel*. Herausgegeben von Ernst Ludwig Enders. (Calw & Stuttgart, 1884 ff.) ("Enders.")
—, *Briefwechsel*. (Weimar, 1930 ff.) ("Briefe.")
—, *Deutsche Bibel* (containing also Luther's prefaces to the Biblical books). (Weimar, 1930 ff.) (WA. "DB.")
—, *Vorlesung ueber den Hebraerbrief* 1517–18. Herausgegeben von Johannes Ficker. (Leipzig, 1929.)

II. Literature on Luther

Alanen, Yrjö J. E., *Das Gewissen bei Luther*. (Helsinki, 1934.)
—, *Tutkimuksia sovitusopin alalta* [Studies on the Doctrine of Atonement] I. (Vaasa, Finland, 1932.)
Augustinus, Aurelius (Augustine), *De civitate Dei* (On the City of God), 413–26.
—, *De correctione et gratia* (On Rebuke and Grace), 426–27.
—, *De doctrinae Christianae* (On Christian Doctrine), 397, 426.
—, *De fide et symbolis* (On Faith and Symbols), 393.
—, *De gratia et libero arbitrio* (On Grace and Free Will), 426–27.
—, *De natura et gratia contra Pelagium* (On Nature and Grace), 415.
—, *De spiritu et littera ad Marcellinum* (On the Spirit and the Letter), 412.
—, *De peccatorum meritis et remissione et de baptismo parvulorum ad Marcellinum* (On Merits and Forgiveness of Sins), 412.
—, *De nuptilis et concupiscentia* (On Marriage and Concupiscence), 419.
—, *Enarrationes in Psalmos* (Commentary on the Psalms), 401–15.
—, *Enchiridion*, 421–422.
—, *Contra secundum Juliani responsionem imperfectum opus* (Against the Second Answer of Julian), 421–29.

Augustinus, *Sermo* XIX and CLIX.
 In references, English names, as indicated in parentheses, are used. Augustine's works are in Migne's *Patrologiae cursus completus, Series Latina*, Volumes 32–45. See the title.
Aulén, Gustaf, *Den kristna gubsbilden genom seklerna och i nutiden* [The Christian Concept of God Through Centuries and in the Present Time]. (Stockholm, 1927.)
Boehmer, Heinrich, *Der junge Luther*. (Gotha, 1925.)
——, *Luther and the Reformation in the Light of Modern Research*. Translated from the fifth German edition by E. S. G. Potter. (London, 1930.) The German title: *Luther im Lichte der neueren Forschung*.
——, *Luthers erste Vorlesung*. (*Berichte ueber die Verhandlungen der Saechsischen Akademie der Wissenschaften zu Leipzig*, Phil. Hist. Kl. Bd. 75, 1923, Leipzig, 1924.)
Bohlin, Torsten, *Gudstro och Kristustro hos Luther* [Faith in God and Christ in Luther's Theology]. (Uppsala, 1927.)
Carlson, Edgar M., *The Reinterpretation of Luther*. (Philadelphia, Pa., 1948.)
Dierks, Theo., "Luther's Spiritual Martyrdom and Its Appeasement." *Concordia Theological Monthly*, XII (1941).
Dobschuetz, Ernst von, "Vom vierfachen Schriftsinn," *Harnack-Ehrung*. (Leipzig, 1921.)
Feckes, Carl, *Die Rechtfertigungslehre des Gabriel Biel*. (Muensterische Beitraege zur Theologie. Muenster i. W., 1925; Roman Catholic.)
Feine, Paul, *Die Erneuerung des Paulinischen Christentums durch Luther*. (Leipzig, 1903.)
Fife, Robert Herndon, *Young Luther. The Intellectual and Religious Development of Martin Luther to 1518*. (New York, 1928.)
Fulgsang-Damgaard, H., "Die Wiederbelebung der Privatbeichte im Lichte der Auffassung Luthers," *Zeitschrift fuer systematische Theologie*. XII (1934).
Grisar, Hartmann, *Luther*, Vol. I. Translated by E. M. Lamond. (St. Louis, Mo., and London, 1913; Roman Catholic.)
——, *Martin Luthers Leben und sein Werk*. (Freiburg im Breisgau, 1926.)
Hahn, Fritz, "Luthers Auslegungsgrundsaetze und ihre theologischen Voraussetzungen," *Zeitschrift fuer systematische Theologie*, XIII (1935).
Hamel, Adolf, *Der junge Luther und Augustin* I–II. (Guetersloh, 1934 and 1935.)
Harnack, Theodosius, *Luthers Theologie* I–II. (New ed. Muenchen, 1927; original ed. 1862.)
Hardeland A., "Der Begriff der *justitia passiva* bei Luther," *Christentum und Wissenschaft*, II (1926).

Bibliography

Hering, Hermann, *Die Mystik Luthers im Zusammenhang mit seiner Theologie und in ihrem Verhaeltnis zur aelteren Mystik.* (Leipzig, 1879.)

Hermann, Rudolph, "Luthers These Gerecht und Suender zugleich," *Zeitschrift fuer systematische Theologie,* VI–VII (1928–29).

Hermelink, H., "Die neuere Lutherdeutung," *Theologische Rundschau,* 1935.

Hirsch, Emanuel, "Initium theologiae Lutheri," *Festgabe fuer Julius Kaftan.* (Tuebingen, 1920.)

Hoffmann, George, "Luther und Melanchthon. Melanchthons Stellung in der Theologie des Luthertums," *Zeitschrift fuer systematische Theologie,* XI (1938).

Holl, Karl, *Gesammelte Aufsaetze zur Kirchengeschichte.* Vol. I, *Luther* (Tuebingen, 1921.) Vol. II. (Tuebingen, 1928.)

——, "Die iustitia Dei in der vorlutherischen Bibelauslegung des Abendlandes," *Festgabe zu A. von Harnack.* (Tuebingen, 1921.) The same also in *op. cit.*

Iwand, Hans Joachim, *Rechtfertigungslehre und Christusglaube. Eine Untersuchung zur Systematik der Rechtfertigungslehre Luthers in ihren Anfaengen.* (Leipzig, 1930.)

Josefson, Ruben, *Oedmjukhet och tro. En studie i den unge Luthers teologi.* [Humility and Faith. A study in the Theology of the Young Luther] (Stockholm, 1939.)

Jundt, André, *Le developpment de la pensée religieuse de Luther jusque'en 1517 d'apres de documents inédites.* (Paris, 1906.)

Kantonen, T. A., *Resurgence of the Gospel.* (Philadelphia, Pa., 1948.)

Kares, Olavi, *Luther I, Henkiloekuva ja kehityssaika.* [Personality and Development]. (Porvoo-Helsinki, 1944.)

Kattenbusch, Ferdinand, "Die vier Formen des Rechtfertigungsgedankens, mit besonderer Ruecksicht auf Luther," *Zeitschrift fuer systematische Theologie,* XI (1933).

Kretzmann, P. E., "Wann und wie kam Luther zur Erkenntnis der Wahrheit?" *Concordia Theological Monthly,* IV (1933).

Kurz, Alfred, *Die Heilsgewissheit bei Luther.* (Guetersloh, 1933.)

Koestlin, Julius, *Luthers Theologie* I–II, 2d ed. (Stuttgart, 1901.)

Ljunggren, Gustaf, *Synd och skuld i Luthers teologi* [Sin and Guilt in Luther's Theology]. (Uppsala, 1928.)

Loofs, Friedrich, *Leitfaden zum Studium der Dogmengeschichte.* (Halle, 1906.)

——, "Justitia Dei passiva in Luthers Anfaengen," *Theologische Studien,* 1911. 1924.

——, "Luthers Rechtfertigungslehre," *Mitteilungen der Luthergesellschaft,* 1924.

——, *Articulus stantis et cadentis ecclesiae,* Theologische Studien und Kritiken, 1917.

Mackinnon, James, *Luther and the Reformation*, Vol. I. *Early Life and Religious Development to 1517.* (London, 1925.) Vol. II. *The Breach with Rome, 1517–21.* (London, 1928.)
Migne, J. P., *Patrologiae cursus completus. . . . Series Latina.* (Paris, 1857 to 1904.)
Mueller, A. V., *Luthers Werdegang bis zum Turmerlebnis.* (Gotha, 1920.)
——, *Luther und Tauler.* (Bern, 1918.)
Nygren, Anders, *Den kristna kaerlekstanken genom tiderna. Eros och Agape.* Vol. II. (Stockholm, 1936.) — Translated into English by Philip S. Watson, 2 vols., with the title, *Agape and Eros. A History of the Christian Idea of Love.* (London and New York, 1938–39.)
——, "Simul iustus et peccator bei Augustin und Luther," *Zeitschrift fuer systematische Theologie,* XVII (1939).
Pinomaa, Lennart, *Der existentielle Charakter der Theologie Luthers.* (Helsinki, 1940.)
——, Luther-tutkielmia [Luther-Studies]. (Helsinki, 1939.)
——, "*Lutherin reformatoorisen murroksen ajankohta*" [The Date of the Reformation Crisis of Luther], *Teologinen Aikakauskirja,* 1941.
Quiring, Horst, "Luther und die Mystik," *Zeitschrift fuer systematische Theologie,* XIV (1936).
Reu, M., *Luther's German Bible. A Historical Presentation Together with a Collection of Sources.* (Columbus, Ohio, 1934.)
Ritschl, Otto, *Dogmengeschichte des Protestantismus.* Vol. II. (Leipzig, 1912.)
Rueckert, Hanns, *Die Rechtfertigungslehre auf dem Tridentinischen Konzil.* (Bonn, 1925.)
Runestam, Arvid, *Den kristliga friheten hos Luther och Melanchthon* [Christian Liberty in the Teaching of Luther and Melanchthon]. (Uppsala, 1917.)
Rupp, Gordon, *Luther's Progress to the Diet of Worms 1521* (SCM Press Ltd., London, 1951.)
Saarnivaara, Uuras, *The Power of the Keys. The Original Faith of the Lutheran Church Presented in Quotation from Luther and the Lutheran Confession.* 2d ed. (Finnish Lutheran Book Concern, Hancock, Michigan, 1945.)
Schaff, Philip, *The Creeds of Christendom, with a History and Critical Notes.* Vol. II: *The Greek and Latin Creeds, with Translations.* (A new edition, New York, 1919.)
Scheel, Otto, *Martin Luther. Vom Katholizismus zur Reformation* I–II. 3d. ed. (Tuebingen, 1921 and 1930.)
Schwiebert, E. G., *Luther and His Times.* (St. Louis, Mo., 1951.)
Seeberg, Erich, *Luthers Theologie, Motive und Ideen.* Vol. II: *Christus Bild und Urbild.* (Stuttgart, 1937.)

Bibliography

Seeberg, Reinhold, *Lehrbuch der Dogmengeschichte*. Vol. II. 3d ed. (Leipzig, 1933.) Vol. IV, 1, 4th ed. (Leipzig, 1933.)
Smith, Preserved, "A Decade of Luther Study," *Harvard Theological Review*, XIV (1921).
——, *The Life and Letters of Martin Luther*. (Boston and New York, 1911.)
Snaith, Norman H., *The Distinctive Ideas of the Old Testament*. (Philadelphia, Pa. 1946.)
Sormunen, Eino, *Jumalan Armo*. Vol. II: *Luther* [God's Grace]. (Helsinki, 1934.) At the end of the book there is a résumé of the contents of the same in the German language.
——, "Mystikan ongelma" [The Problem of Mysticism], *Vartija*, No. 11–12, 1933, and No. 2, 1934.
Staupitz, Johann von, *Tuebinger Predigten*, Edited by G. Buchwald and Ernst Wolf. (Leipzig, 1927.)
Stracke, Ernst, *Luthers grosses Selbstzeugnis 1545 ueber seine Entwicklung zum Reformator*. (Schriften des Vereins der Reformationsgeschichte, No. 140, Leipzig, 1926.)
Strohl, Henri, *L'evolution religieuse de Luther jusqu'en 1515*. (Strasbourg & Paris, 1922.)
Tapaninen, P. E., *Lutherin Kirkkonaekemys* [Luther's Idea of the Church]. (Kemi, Finland, 1942.)
Tauler, Johann, *Predigten I–III*. (Frankfurt am Main, 1926.)
Thieme, K., *Die sittliche Triebkraft des Glaubens*. (Leipzig, 1895.)
Thimme, Hans, *Christi Bedeutung fuer Luthers Glauben, unter Zugrundelegung des Roemerbriefs, des Hebraeerbriefs, des Galaterbriefkommentars von 1531 und der Disputationen*. (Guetersloh, 1933.)
Vogelsang, Erich, *Die Anfaenge von Luthers Christologie nach der ersten Psalmenvorlesung, insbesondere in ihren exegetischen und systematischen Zusammenhaengen mit Augustin und der Scholastik dargestellt*. (Arbeiten zur Kirchengeschichte, XV. Berlin und Leipzig, 1929.)
——, *Unbekannte Fragmente aus Luthers zweiter Psalmenvorlesung*. (Berlin, 1940.)
——, "Luther und Mystik," *Luther-Jahrbuch*, XIX. (Weimar, 1929.)
Walter, Johannes von, "Der Abschluss der Entwicklung des jungen Luther," *Zeitschrift fuer systematische Theologie*, I (1923).
Watson, Philip S., *Let God Be God. An Interpretation of the Theology of Martin Luther*, (London-Philadelphia, Pa., 1948.)
Weber, Hans Emil, *Reformation, Orthodoxie und Rationalismus* I. (Guetersloh, 1937.)
Wendorf, Hermann, "Der Durchbruch der neuen Erkenntnis Luthers im Lichte der handschriftlichen Ueberlieferung," *Historische Vierteljahrschrift*, XXVI (1932).

Wolf, Ernst, *Staupitz und Luther. Ein Beitrag zur Theologie des Johannes von Staupitz und deren Bedeutung fuer Luthers theologischen Werdegang.* (Quellen und Forschungen zur Reformationsgeschichte, IX, Leipzig, 1927.)

——, "Ueber neuere Lutherliteratur und den Gang der Lutherforschung," *Christentum und Wissenschaft*, IX, (1933).

Wolff, Otto, *Die Haupttypen der neueren Lutherdeutung.* (Tuebinger Studien zur systematischen Theologie, Stuttgart, 1938.)

Index

Abbild, 61
Absolution, 27—28, 33, 106, 121
Active justice or righteousness, XIII, 16, 39, 41, 43, 44, 64, 66, 112, 113
Alanen, Yrjö J. E., 27, 91, 133
Alien righteousness, *aliena iustitia*, 83, 86, 92, 93, 95, 97
Ambrosiaster, 40
Amorbach, 131
Analytic proposition, 64, 82
Archetype, 61—62
Areopagite, 75, 118
Aristotle, 90
Arndt, William, X
Assurance of salvation, 44, 46, 47, 86, 98, 107, 119
Attritio, 23
Augustine, Augustinian, XV, 3—9, 14 to 18, 25, 37, 40, 43, 53—55, 61 to 63, 66—72, 74, 78, 82, 84, 91, 95, 99, 103, 105, 106, 109—11, 114, 115, 120, 121, 123, 127, 130, 132.
Augustinian Friars, Monks, XV, 27, 32, 57

Baptism, 4, 29
Bernhard of Clairvaux, 25, 75, 121
Biel, Gabriel, 25, 27, 30, 42, 55
Boehmer, Heinrich, 25, 26, 29, 34, 48, 59, 74, 105, 112, 130
Bohlin, Torsten, 26, 30, 32, 68, 73
Bonaventura, 75
Bridget (Birgitta), 75

Caritas (charity, love), 4, 5, 7
Calvinistic, 17
Carlson, Edgar M., 91

Certainty of salvation, see *Assurance of salvation*
Change of taste, 9, 15
Charles V, 37
Chicago, University of, X
Church, 119—120
Clemen, O., 112
Compensatory view of justification, 18
Concupiscence, 4, 79 (see also *Evil lust*)
Confession (of sins), 23—27, 29, 30, 57
Conformity of Christ, *conformitas Christi*, 24, 75, 116
Conscience, 21—25, 29, 31, 36, 75, 76, 113
Conversion, 15, 22, 46, 114, 122, 123

Denifle, H., 40, 70
Devotio moderna, 25
Dierks, Theo., 29
Dikaioo, 15
Discovery of evangelical insight into justification, XV, 34—49, 70, 101 to 103, 114 (see also *Tower experience*)
Disposition (preparedness, fitness), to grace, 22, 23, 63
Disputations, academic, of Wittenberg, 11, 13
Dobschuetz, E. von, 60

Erasmus, 74
Erfurt, 25, 27, 30, 57
Ethical view of justification, 85—86 (see also *Active justice or righteousness*)

143

Evil lust, 4, 9 (see also *Concupiscence*)
Example, 62, 117
Exegesis, modern, 14
Experience, religious, 46—47, 124
Expurgation (of sin), 13

Faber Stapulensis (LeFevre d' Etable), 60—62
Fall (into sin), 4
Fanatics, 119—120
Feckes, C., 27
Feine, Paul, 15
Ficker, Joh., 74, 134
Fife, R. H., 34, 42, 48
Finland, X
Flesh and spirit, 85—86
Fourteen Consolations, a book of Luther, 1519, 99—100
Fruits of faith, XIV, 13, 14, 15
Fuglsang-Damgaard, H., 27

Galatians, Luther's early lectures (1516—17) and Commentary on it (1519), 36, 88, 103—104, 107
Galatians, Luther's later Large Commentary on it (1535), 32, 42, 60, 61, 117
Galgenrew (*attritio*), 23
Gelassenheit, 75—76
Genesis, Luther's Commentary on it, 20
German Theology, *Theologia germanica*, 75, 118, 132
Gerson, 75
Graebner, Theodore, X
Gratia — donum, 11, 83, 117
Great testimony, Luther's, see *Preface*
Grisar, H., 49, 70, 119—120

Hahn, Fritz, 60, 116
Hamel, Adolf, 40, 61, 62, 63, 66, 73, 110, 130, 132, 134, 135

Hardeland, A., 40, 44
Harnack, Theodosius, 49
Hebrews, Epistle to the, Luther's lectures on it, 36, 88, 98, 107
Heidelberg, disputation of, 90—91
Helsinki, 10
Hering, H., 118
Hermelink, H., 129
Hirsch, Emanuel, 47, 48, 59, 63, 64, 73, 112, 135
Holl, Karl, Hollian, XV, 9, 13, 40, 44, 72, 82, 87, 91
Hugo of St. Victor, 75
Huss, John, 122, 124
Hypocaustum, 37, 48

Inner repentance, 27
Iustitia Dei, see *Righteousness of God*
Iustum facere, 15 (see also *Justification and sanctification, relations between*)
Iwand, H. J., 49, 63, 129

Josefson, Ruben, 86—87
Jundt, André, 26
Justification, instantaneous, 10
Justification and sanctification, relation between, 11—18, 14, 63, 70 to 72, 78—117, 123
"Justification of God," 62—63, 113

Kantonen, T. A., 82
Kattenbusch, F., 18
Kempis, Thomas à, 25
Knaake, J. F., 128—129
Koestlin, Julius, 30
Kukkonen, Walter J., X
Kurz, Alfred, 47, 49

Lang, Johann, 95
Law and Gospel, relationship between, 12, 13, 16, 43—46, 68—71, 78, 85, 119
Law, Ceremonial, 70, 74

Index

Law, Moral, 70, 75
Law of God (in general), 4, 6, 9, 12, 16, 29, 38, 43, 45
Law, written in the heart, 12
LeFevre, see *Faber Stapulensis*
Leipzig, disputation of, 107
Liberal theology, IX
Lindroth, Hjalmar, 87
Ljunggren, Gustaf, 91, 129
Literary heritage of Luther, 125–126
Loewenich, Walter von, 91
Lombard, Peter, 34, 40, 53, 54, 56, 109, 130
Loofs, Fr., 40, 44, 48, 63
Lund, school of, Lundensianism, 91
Luther Renaissance, IX
Lutheran Orthodoxy, 18, 87

Mackinnon, James, 46, 48, 111–112, 132
Melanchthon, 87, 133
Metanoia, metanoein, 20
Migne, J. P., 127, 130, 131
Miltitz, Karl von, 35, 104, 107, 108
Monastery of Wittenberg, 48, 116
Mueller, A. V., 27, 49, 59, 132
Mysticism, Mystics, 25, 62, 71, 75 to 76, 118–119, 121–122, 124, 132

Neo-Platonism, Neo-Platonic, 8, 61, 69
Ninety-five Theses, Luther's, 35, 88
Nitsch, 76
Nominalism, Nominalists, 25, 27, 30, 32, 55 (see also *Occamism, Occam,* and *Biel, Gabriel*)
Nygren, Anders, 47, 127

Obedience and justification, 11–12
Occamism, Occam, 25, 55, 71, 130
October 19, 1512, 56, 58

Paltz, Johann, 25
Paradise, 36, 43, 106

"Passive" righteousness and justification, XIV, 15, 40–45
Pattern, 61–62, 68, 117
Pauck, Wilhelm, X
Pelagian, 3
Penitential Psalms, Luther's Commentary on, 88–89
Philosophical view of righteousness, 112, 114
Pinomaa, Lennart, 49, 76, 113–114
Place of Tower Experience, 37, 48
Platonic, 118
Predestination, 8, 20, 21, 24, 30–34, 39, 70
Preface, Luther's, to his works 1545, 35, 37, 41, 45, 55, 97, 98, 104–105, 108, 109, 111, 114, 122
Principles of the Reformation, formal and material, 124
Psalms, Luther's first lectures on (1513–15), 34, 36, 58–73, 104
Psalms, Luther's second series of lectures on (1519–21), 98–99, 102 to 104, 108, 111, 115
Psalm 31:2, 45, 64, 93, 96, 99, 115
Psalm 71:2, 49, 64, 66, 72
Psalterium quintuplex, 60

Quadriga, or fourfold Scripture sense, 60–62, 77, 89, 115–116, 118
Quiring, H., 61, 118, 132

Reconciliatory view of justification, 18
Reparatory view of justification, 18
Repentance, 4, 19, 20, 22–29, 113
Reputare iustum, 67, 72, 99
Retributory order of salvation, 25
Reu, M., 48, 130
Richard of St. Victor, 75
Righteousness of God, *iustitia Dei*, 36–46, 55, 64, 65, 66, 71, 93, 96, 98–102, 105, 106, 112, 114, 115

Romans 1:16-17, 36–47, 55, 73, 96, 108, 111, 115, 117, 122
Roman Catholic Church, doctrine, and theology, IX, 17, 23, 26, 27, 28, 29, 32, 41, 43, 44, 47, 55, 64, 70, 104, 106, 115, 118, 119, 122
Romans, Luther's lecture on, 43, 46, 49, 62, 74–87, 107, 109, 118
Rome, Luther's journey to, 57
Rueckert, Hans, 17
Runestam, Arvid, 133, 134
Rupp, Gordon, 49, 125

Saarnivaara, Uuras, 27
Sacraments, 27, 119–120
Samaritan, 66, 79
Sanative justification, 110 (see also *Justification and sanctification, relation between*)
Savonarola, 124
Shadow – reality, 69
Schaff, Philip, 17
Scheel, Otto, 25, 26, 27, 29, 30, 33, 34, 44, 73, 129, 130, 135
Schwaermerisch, 119, 120
Schwiebert, E. G., 49, 135
"Second righteousness," 12, 92–98
Seeberg, Erich, 135
Seeberg, Reinhold, 91, 116
Seelengrund, 76
Semi-Pelagianism, 3, 32
Simul iustus et peccator, simultaneously righteous and sinful, 7, 80
Sittler, Joseph, X
Smith, Preserved, 49
Sormunen, Eino, 25, 48, 135
Spalatin, Georg, 59, 109, 132
Staupitz, Johann von, XV, 19–34, 39, 45, 53, 54, 56–58, 88, 106, 121, 128
Stracke, Ernst, 11

Strohl, Henri, 33
Syneidesis, conscience, 76
Synteresis, 76–77, 113

Table Talks, of Luther, 21, 37, 42
Tappert, Theodore G., 130
Tauler, Johann, 75, 76, 133
Tetzel, 35, 107, 108
Theologia crucis, theology of the cross, 116–117
Theologia germanica, see *German Theology*
Threefold righteousness, 92–95
Tower Experience and discovery 35 to 48, 56–57, 69, 71–73, 92, 101 to 109, 114, 122–123 (see also *Discovery of evangelical insight into justification*)
Trent, Council of, 17
Tropological interpretation and sense of Scripture, 60–61, 65, 68, 115, 116, 118
Trutvetter, 54
Twilight period of the Reformation, 122
Twofold righteousness, 95–98

Urbild, 61, 117

Vergeltungsordnung, 25
Vogelsang, Erich, 33, 44, 48, 59, 62, 64, 65, 66, 71–73, 102, 118, 132
Vulgate, 58, 116

Walter, Johannes von, 47, 48, 107, 112
Watson, Philip S., 33, 47, 49, 127
Weber, H. E., 120
Wendorf, H., 48, 59, 72–73, 132
Wittenberg, University of, 11, 13, 25, 118
Wolf, Ernst, 47, 57, 128, 129
Wolff, Otto, 126, 135
Wycliffe, 122, 124

www.ingramcontent.com/pod-product-compliance
Lightning Source LLC
Chambersburg PA
CBHW051107160426
43193CB00010B/1351